# Key Account Management in Pharma

## A comprehensive compendium

**ISBN: 978 375 3458 762**

9 783753 458762

*"The centerpiece of Key Account Management is the creation of lasting and robust relationships between businesses."*

# Preface

*Key Account Management in Pharma* is designed to define, clarify, guide, and support readers around a promising business-to-business-model for the pharmaceutic industry. Managers in the pharmaceutical industry appear to have widely different understandings of what this acronym and the underlying business-model stands for. Even inside the same organisation, more often than not it is unclear what these three letters "KAM" really mean or could mean.

Many aspects in the settings of markets of the pharmaceutical industry have changed in recent years. Changes are gathering momentum and the speed of change is accelerating. The theory of evolution tells us that those who are most adaptive to change, will survive. In the pharmaceutical industry's ecosystem, we have seen several *species* which have already become extinct. Additionally, mergers and acquisitions are continuously reducing the number of companies alive.

Spoiled by a wealthy past, some celebrate their reluctance to change. They stay where and what they are. Prof. Brian D. Smith wrote in his article "The end of Pharma" *Some parts of our industry may go the way of the kitchen display cabinet and the word processor"*[1]

Pharma has been exposed to more legal and regulatory restrictions in recent years. Compulsory codes of conduct have been rolled-out after

---

[1] www.pmlive.com, Pharmaceutical Market Europe, November 2019

fines amounting to billions of dollars had been paid by pharma for misbehaviour in marketing and sales.

Technological developments carrying a tag called "digital", add to complexity causing even more challenges in this digital-adverse industry. Actively introducing and driving Key Account Management as a methodology can open numerous windows of opportunity.

In the past the pharmaceutical industry missed to actively shape what we tend to call the "pharmaceutical market". After the central characteristic of a market is the presence of *demand and supply* there had not even been a market in the narrow economic sense of the word in the past. The demand side still is missing in some countries. Examples? With regards to Rx-drugs, patients cannot execute demand owed to missing the necessary knowledge and the right to purchase without prescription. Prescribing physicians are mediators, prescribing an available, listed medication. Payers, i.e. insurances or tax-funded reimbursement-organisations compensate for products prescribed. Pharma is the supplier, but who stands for the demand side?

Pharma still is caught in *selling* to their *customers* when they mean promoting a drug to a prescribing physician. They call these prescribers *customers*.

The word *customer* is defined as "Someone who bought or purchased (in the past-tense) a product or service." Buying and selling" is a transactional business, an exchange of a product, service, or rights against money. Considering this, applying the word customer to a physician at least is misleading and leading towards misconduct.

Traditional habits prevail even after "selling" never resulted in a transaction. In the past, terms like "sales force" or "selling" have lead training companies, HR-departments, marketers, and medical reps far astray. Astray form their original decent: being a helpful and supportive therapeutic advisor to their target audience. What a pharmaceutical field force pursues is **non**-transactional. This means that *selling* and *buying* do not happen.

> *"Selling, deal-closing and negotiation-skills"-courses for medical reps have contributed a lot to pharma's poor reputation.*

The simple introduction of the word "selling" into pharmaceutical field-forces in the early 1980s drove senior management, field force mentalities, and mindsets into a wrong direction. It mis-shaped business processes, reduced rep's education, and led to the share of voice model.

Until 2021, respecting needs and requirements of prescribing physicians is widely disregarded or only little more than a lip service.

> *You do not need to be a pessimist to worry about the ability of the industry to adapt to the future.*

The number of pharmaceutical companies is getting smaller. Mergers, acquisitions and deliberate bankruptcies[2] take their toll from the overall number of companies. Larger pharma companies frequently acquire smaller companies or medical start-ups with specific abilities. Small entities often have a single remedy in phase II or III. Specialists or rare-disease units are major targets.

Patent protection and fully exploited pricing ranges make such companies valuable assets for their bigger peers. Therapy cost of million Euro or more, no longer establish a threshold for

---

[2] https://www.statnews.com/2019/09/16/if-purdue-pharma-declares-bankruptcy-what-would-it-mean-for-lawsuits-against-the-opioid-manufacturer/

reimbursement. Of course, access to the market, registration and granted reimbursement are the determining factors. A single physician plays a marginal role. Pharma's targets for Rx-drugs today are organisations or legal bodies. Tender businesses dominate many markets. My first contact with tender business was in Saudi-Arabia in early 2002. In the Kingdom of Saudi-Arabia submissions for drugs had regularly been requested by the military, being the major healthcare provider.

In Germany, the prescription market is dominated by tender business as well. In the largest of the EU-5 markets, 80% of all prescriptions are generic. Not to be thought of 20 years ago.

Statutory health insurances cover about 85% of the population. They invite for submissions granting business for 24 months, sometimes exclusively. Most contractual agreements are shared between up to three providers. The only differentiator in these markets currently is the cost of a pillbox. Following sources familiar with the procedure, confidentially granted rebates reach up to 90% from the list price. Bound to a European cost-structure, such pricing cannot be profitable for an enterprise nor grant survival.

Given such a setting the old-fashioned sales-model of pharma appears unsustainable. Contracts "decide" which product is to be prescribed. Pharmacists are obliged to substitute accordingly, and chronically ill patients are used to receiving changing pill-packs with different names and colours. In such a scenario visiting physicians with a field force does not really make sense any longer.

*Key Account Management may be one entry door into another era of pharma's prosperity.*

# Why this book?

First a clarification what this book will **not** deliver:

It is not a cookbook, reciting benchmarks, showing so-called best practices, making anyone believe that following others guarantees success.

The book's idea:

The book intends to share ideas and point towards conceptual Key Account Management approaches, most probably helpful for the mid-term future. Ensuring a common understanding, needs a defined and common, yet versatile, vocabulary applied and spoken in Key Account Management.

The book is rooted in 45 years of experience in the pharmaceutical industry's world. Discussions, meetings, events, and deep experiences with pharmaceutical professionals in more than 25 countries on all continents are a sound basis. Writing was a challenge, considering different countries, different markets, different settings of healthcare systems in general with varying payers.

In the majority of countries, both in developed and emerging markets, the traditional sales model of the pharma industry appears to be moribund, if not yet already dead. In 2012 Booz & Company (worldwide, National Analysts, booz&co , 2012) published these survey results:

*68% of respondents believed that the current pharmaceutical model is broken and needs significant repair. Fewer than 10% believe the model is not broken.*

Pharma exported their traditional sales- and business-model from developed markets into emerging-market countries. Owed to globalization and shared experiences across continents, the learning curves today are much steeper in those recently established marketplaces. It took 30 years of pharma's efforts to end the "race or arms" of field force size and numbers of calls. The underlying "share of voice model" will fade out in the emerging markets a lot faster, than it did in the developed markets. Additionally, in almost all countries, pharmaceutical products nowadays are marketed in a true market surrounding.

Economists will remember what "market" stands for:

*Market* is "one of a composition of systems, institutions, procedures, social relations or infrastructures whereby parties engage in exchange." Market means to deliberately bring demand and supply together.

- There are drug companies, which offer **supply**, and there are commercial and professional entities which stand for **demand**.
  Demand can come from a state or governmental tender, a national health system, Medicare, Medicaid, PBM, the NHS, PCTs, distributors, hospital- or pharmacy-chains and many other possible networks or legal entities.
- In contrast to the individual prescriber, in all these entities, decision making depends and relies on several people. No one establishes a decision by himself.

In numerous projects we found that the acronym KAM was used indicating different things and concepts. In the 2020s the term KAM is still used as the better sounding notion, often applied to a re-named hospital salesforce of the past.

This is the definition of the "technical term" **ACCOUNT**:

> *An account is an entity, group, or network of people in which*
> *decisions about drugs, devices or services are made by*
> *several people.*

## KEY ACCOUNT MANAGEMENT IN PHARMA

Kotler's marketing concepts started with product centricity, evolved to customer centricity and currently we talk, learn and read about Marketing 3.0. *"From products to customers to the human spirit."*

Making Key Account Management future proof will need an underlying philosophy, much more holistic and imminently involved in the delivery of healthcare. KAM is a lot more than selling pillboxes at a price. From experience, you can tell that procedures and market approaches of the past will not withstand the omnipresent political pressures.

The challenge is to establish Key Account Management as a novel business model.

# Content

# FUTURE HAS A PAST

After I started working in the pharma field force in 1975 in Germany, colleagues shared with me plenty of their experiences in the pharmaceutical area in these days and the time before mine.

At the restart of the German economy in the 1950ies, the number and locations of medical practices were limited and fully regulated. Not all of the physicians therefore could find a place to settle and open their own medical practice in these days. After these practices had been established, pharmaceutical companies invented a personalized channel to inform prescribing physicians about the therapeutic state-of-the-art and their products.

Pharma started hiring, educating, and sending pharmaceutical advisors to doctors in their private practice.

In these early days, "pharmaceutical advisors" have usually been medical doctors themselves and they started visiting their colleagues to tell them how to treat a specific disease and use or administer a specific drug.

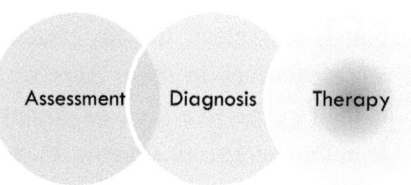

**EXHIBIT 1: A MANAGERIAL "TRIPLE JUMP"**

If the pharmaceutical advisor was not a physician himself, at least he needed to be a pharmacist, i.e. a member of the health care guild.

Only people with such a background, a reasonable degree of seniority and high trustworthiness could discuss, advise, and listen to doctors being on par with their colleagues in the office or a hospital ward.

To differentiate from these non-prescription OTC drugs, prescription drugs were called "ethical drugs". It was perceived unethical to request, talk or press a physician into prescribing or using "my" drug.

Whenever there was a good reason to advise the prescription of another company's medicine, this was fine and fully in line with the professional goals and ethics.

If a doctor needed advice or assistance in his therapeutic decisions, pharmaceutical advisors have been the perfect source of knowledge, displaying common medical sense, carrying wisdom and experiences from knowing plenty of other colleagues, having intimate insight into many doctor offices.

The doctor's own and fully respected domain consisted of the steps:

- assessing and examining a patient
- finding a diagnosis.

After diagnosis was clear, therapy was the next step. The claim of medical representatives in these days was a deep knowledge about therapy in their respective area of competence. They had a deeper knowledge in the therapeutical arena, than a "normal" physician could have. Owed to their education and usually seeing 10 physicians a day, they could share any experience even around endemic illnesses.

When one of those medical representatives knocked at the door, in many cases the doctor asked his nurse to close the office, keep patients away and allow him half an hour discussing with the advisor from well-reputed pharmaceutical companies. Coffee and cookies offered by the doctor have been somewhat standard. The doctor sometimes felt honoured, being important enough to be visited.

In contrast to today, the word "customer" was obsolete. Words as selling etc. did not even exist and calls were called "visits" and lasted around 15 minutes and longer on average.

Doctors saw these visits as a perfect break in their every-day office hours. They could refrain from asking and listening to patients. Instead of they could share, talk, and exchange at peer-level. Doctors enjoyed the break, being encouraged to ask questions, and receive valued and valuable advice from their therapeutic advisors, later called medical representatives in return.

*Those were the days, my friend.*

# THERAPY ADVISOR OR SALES REP

It was in the early 1980's, when words like *sales, selling* or *sales force* had been introduced into the profession of the pharmaceutical representative. Pharma's "only living contact to physicians" was put into a new and different pair of shoes.

The everyday life of the former "therapy advisor" changed considerably: the transition from advisors, respected consultants with rich knowledge, carrying a lot of therapeutical experience and delivering value to physicians, to becoming sales people, had begun.

Medical representatives started a metamorphosis.

One of the drivers of changes in their "sense-of-self and in the profession was the availability of "sales data". With the availability of these data, the objectives of pharma changed. "Creating a preference" to prescribe my drug, driven by value, delivered through reps was gone. The era of revenue and market share started.

In 1972 IMS Health became a publicly listed company and in 1973 Medical Communications and Life Sciences divisions have been formed. At the beginning of the "era of selling", every company had established their own market intelligence. Market data, the comparison with competitors, the size of an indication area etc. have been heavily used from product managers and forecasters around the world. Increased granularity of data and the option to look into sales at a brick level drove change and the desire to hold reps accountable for creating revenue.

This was a starting point of monitoring and auditing pharmaceutical sales and one of the tipping points for "pharmaceutical advisors". More and more they were converted into "salespeople". The fashion of setting sales objectives started.

Huge and heavy sales reports, 100s of pages of "tractor-fed" paper, printed with the first laser printers, contained data of a quarter, my own product and its competitors and of a group of reps. Computers still were of the size of a 3-bedroom apartment and the paper printed was measured in tons, transported by mail to regional managers.

*The physician and his needs ceased to be of relevance for marketing and sales in the pharmaceutical industry.*

First line and senior managers started talking about revenue of a drug achieved or missing; they judged on their sub-ordinates following gains and losses and held them responsible for missing revenue. The quality of a rep from now on was measured in sales, sales increase, market share, market share increase or any kind of index made from these numbers.

The good rep from now on was the one with high sales.

The quality of their advice, their often intimate, professional relationship with prescribers, the deep knowledge about disease and drug, their ability to differentiate their advice according to the person in front of them, did no longer count. Asking the doctor for feedback and adding value to every minute of the doctor's time no longer was an appreciated feature. The time of a professional link between community physicians through knowledgeable and trustworthy reps from the pharmaceutical industry ended.

**The industry's business model still is the same until today: Promote drugs to prescribers and make them prescribe.**

# SELLING-SKILLS

Senior and other managers still are using the old vocabulary, attempting to tweak and redefine meaning and perception. It often looks and sounds like "riding a dead horse".

*"It is important to understand the current definition of selling, and in pharma that continues to be primarily 'message delivery' – and usually a product message at that - and certainly that needs to change."* (Paul Simms, 2014)

The problem in above quote from an eyeforpharma paper is that "selling" to a doctor hardly is defined, let alone does the act of pharma's selling match the "normal" perception or economic rules.

Selling in principle is a transaction, an exchange of a product, a right, or a service against money[3]. *Selling* is understood in this way across the world. Using the term *selling* in the context with a rep's activity therefore is wrong. In addition, we must admit that "selling" nowadays has a negative connotation, at least with the people who are sold to.

This has changed, when markets evolved from being seller's markets in the times of short supply to the buyer's markets we live in today. Buyer's markets: abundant supply, a huge variety of each product at almost any time and place, is today's situation.

In the past, pharmaceutical companies trained their people in sales techniques, such as Spin-Selling[4] etc. Core of these trainings was the

---

[3] https://www.merriam-webster.com/dictionary/selling
[4] https://en.wikipedia.org/wiki/Neil_Rackham

identification of the call flow and the steps within this flow to be executed during each call.

Selling skills training was about a clear sequence of steps which have been monitored by rep's managers. Their job was to assess and improve the degree of call-flow execution. In most cases and across almost all pharmaceutical companies the steps have been the same, training companies were the same and the outcome did not vary between companies.

MedReps had been trained to sell their products to counterparts that never bought or buy anything: prescribing physicians.

In today's world, the vocabulary used appears to be outdated and words like *negotiating* or *closing a deal* point into aspects, which could cause expensive infringements of legal frameworks. Companies listed at the New York Stock Exchange fear the in-call behaviours of medical reps trained this way. In 2020, Purdue Pharma[5] is well known for being under heavy scrutiny about their sales campaigns for Oxycontin. A Massachusetts attorney general complained in her multi-billion US$ lawsuit that members of the Sackler family are "personally responsible". She alleges they micromanaged a "deceptive sales campaign."

Preparation
↓
Opening
↓
Probing
↓
Positioning the brand
↓
Handling objections
↓
Gaining commitment
↓
Post-call review

**EXHIBIT 2: TYPICAL CALL FLOW**

---

[5] https://en.wikipedia.org/wiki/Purdue_Pharma

Many "sales-reps" have been employed neglecting the facts that Coleman et al. had published already in 1966:

*"This important individual is a salesman who does not sell, just as the doctor is a customer who does not buy...The paying customer, of course, is the patient who takes his prescription to the pharmacist"* (Coleman, Medical Innovation. A diffusion study, 1966)

# THE „RACE OF ARMS"

Once selling as a concept was introduced and adopted by pharma, their field-forces were renamed and since then called salesforces.

The salesforce was fighting to achieve the planned launch trajectory, market share, or revenue with new launches at short intervals. Frequent new products caused short launch intervals requiring higher numbers of contacts. Pharma tried the obvious and increased the expected or demanded number of calls per day and the call frequency per doctor.

Medical reps, having lost their ethos as therapeutical advisors, very early smelled the new "piece-rate". They successfully hindered their managers from turning this screw endlessly. It was easy to tell and pretend that more calls per day are not possible.

The option to increase "days in the field" therefore showed limited impact, but anyway: meetings had been reduced in number and duration. Training of any kind was carefully weighed against "days in field" lost as a downside of education.

Contact frequency became the Holy Grail of pharma sales and marketing.

In these days, being loaded with money, the next option for the pharmaceutical industry was to increase the number of reps. In order to interfere with existing relationships as little as possible, most of these "sales-force structure" and alignment-projects followed the concept of adding more sales lines. It was no longer one representative selling specific drugs, but *"My range of products has become so wide that I needed assistance. From next week on you will be visited by a new colleague of mine as well."* was one of the standard announcements and excuses, when a physician asked the rep he knew best.

In these days, the doctor still had the right to select his drug of choice. He had the power to decide which drug to prescribe. Pressing new drugs into a more and more crowded market, needed more than one rep and more than 10 calls a day. It needed a second line, duplicating *sales capacity* and add pressure on the prescribing physician. Once the dam was broken and a second line of reps was hired and trained, it was a logical step to add more. In the late 80s to mid-90s there were companies having six and more sales-lines on the street. When a new product needed to be launched, it was normal that all these sales lines and reps promoted the same product. Call frequency went up to once a week or even more often and the patience of physicians was set to test the limits. The total number of medical reps in some countries went up to one rep per doctor in office.

Even in 2020 there still is one of the biggest pharma companies in Germany deploying three sales lines, promoting the same core product to a widely overlapping target group of prescribers.

## SHARE OF VOICE

Throughout the 90s and the early years of the new millennium, this "race of arms" was the gold standard. The underlying concept was simple, the results clear: there was an almost linear correlation between the number of calls / the share of voice and the market share achieved. Many market data providers and consultants published and stated evidence for a cause-effect between share of voice and share of market.

## PHARMA'S INSIDE-OUT PERSPECTIVE

The mentality of pharma marketing and sales was seen as selfish or egoistic. The only thing that counted was the reach of the salesforce and the achieved call frequency. It was the blockbuster era. Imagine that in the 90ies the global pharma market was growing double digit. In 1999, the US market alone went up by 17%. The gold rush around the so-called emerging markets had not even started. Growing sales was assumed to be the direct result of salesforces and nothing was sweeter than revenue. Double-digit growth rates have been normal. Plans and forecasts did not allow anything other than this. Such mentality neglects what physicians in their offices or in hospitals say or think. Statements like "need-detection" have been nothing than lip-services in training courses. Ask any question, but think about the mandatory marketing message, when replying. It was all about hammering the marketing message x-times per visit into the doctor's mind and alter his prescribing habits in favour of the promoted product.

To achieve this, unethical or law-breaking habits were and sometimes still are endemic in marketing and sales in some countries. Bribery, sometimes hidden behind the wall of medical education, still is seen as being rather normal. Misstatements and off-label promotion were used to gain market share by almost all means. Reps had to make their sales targets. An article (2014) was published about the situation. This quote is taken from the British Journal of Medicine (BMJ 2014;348:g3169 , 2014):

*There is also widespread corruption in the pharmaceutical industry, with doctors bribed to prescribe particular drugs.*

"Customer needs" was an unknown species. As long as p=0,005, everything was significant, and the product usually was called "best-in-class" and "new". Generics often were branded to pretend novelty or differentiation. Bioavailability was one of the key words invented and used by almost everyone to show equality over *originals.*

Big pharma was happy, kind of relaxed and bottom-line profits anyway have been and still are a lot higher than in most other industries.

# Pharma: resting in itself

We are fine, our growth is perfect, top and bottom line are exceptional; our people sell, we are happy and want to remain happy: Do not disturb!

In the 21st century's first decade the industry slowly understood that governments, payers, and healthcare providers felt something like "enough is enough".

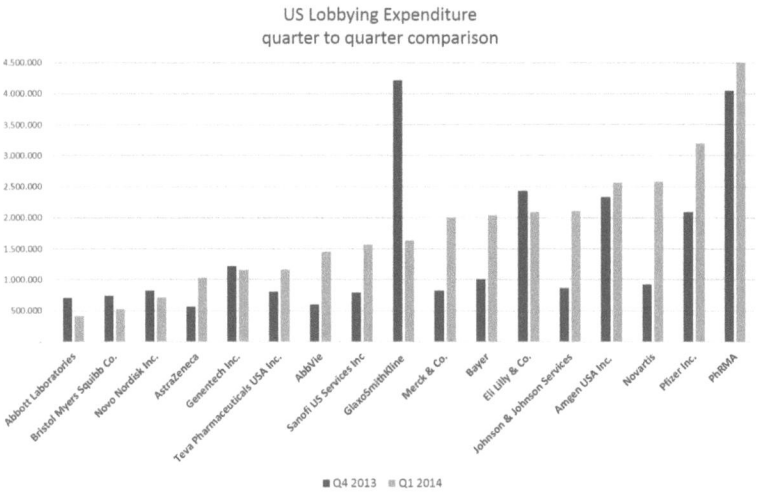

**EXHIBIT 3: DEVELOPMENT OF LOBBYING EXPENDITURE IN THE US (COOPER, 2014)**

In 2019 Pfizer, Johnson & Johnson, Merck, and the other major drug makers belong to PhRMA, together spent more than $120 million lobbying Congress.[6] This is $ 10 million per month.

Political lobbying is designed to influence political decision making. But when an industry sits and waits for lawmakers to act, the outcome hardly can be favourable.

In many cases and countries pharma's lobbying did not work in the past and hardly will have beneficial effects in the future. One of the major reasons for predicted failure is missing trust in pharma. In addition, "gambling", or bargaining with number of employees or job-losses etc. is not a valid point. Even politicians today know that the number of jobs in pharma in many countries is small, compared with the total number of jobs in healthcare. Take Germany as an example: in 2017 about 83 million inhabitants have 5.6 Mio people work in the health care sector. Pharma employs around 121,000 people. This means that pharma employs 0,02% of all those, making a living in healthcare.

---

[6] https://www.statnews.com/2020/01/23/lobbying-drug-pricing-receipts/

OECD data about the total health care expenditure as a percentage of GDP indicate that the political will is to reduce cost of care as a share of GDP.

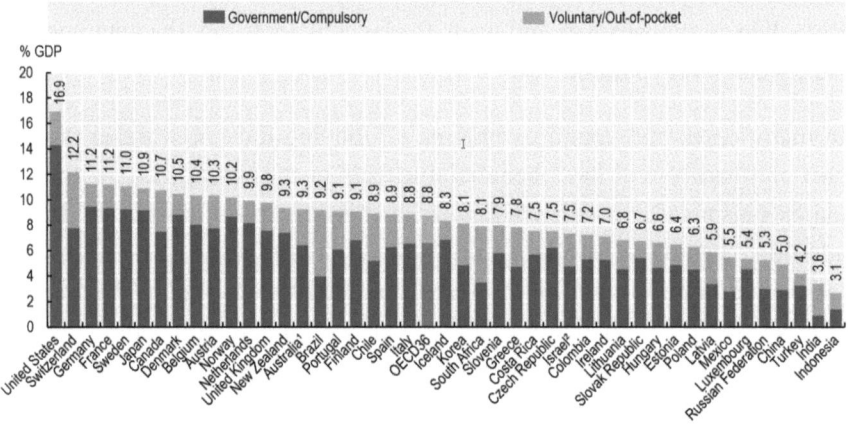

Figure 7.3. **Health expenditure as a share of GDP, 2018 (or nearest year)**

**EXHIBIT 4: OECD DATA**

The lever for the reduction of total cost does not really lie in the prices of medicines, but price pressure sends a signal to all involved in health care, especially impacting voters.

Politically it is a good idea to press pharma since this industry is not the most trusted one. The voting public appreciates putting the blame on a rich industry. Drug prices and drug companies simply appear to be the *locus minoris resistentiae*, the area of least resistance, on the political map of power.

The lasting problem is that lawmakers decide like politicians always do: in a political way. This means that political decisions must not follow subject matter expertise. Political decisions made by politicians are usually made for their voters to ensure re-election.

A valid general assumption is that the political will is to limit health care cost to a certain percentage of GDP. In India this is around 4% of GDP and in Germany this figure currently is around 11%. The numbers vary by country but in most countries, pharma's hope for more is based on growing GDP. Higher gains in top-line revenue will rather come from shifts between current treatments to more efficient or more costly medication.

In principle, the political decision-making pattern will tend to squeeze more money out of the pharma industry and pretend that this political activity could prevent the total cost of healthcare to rise.

The pharmaceutical industry being a major target, will probably prevail if pharma is trying to *sell* products to customers who do not buy, because it coincides with and triggers missing trust. This is nourished by the industry's pricing policy, being hardly comprehensible. One recent example is Zolgensma® by Novartis. A product to treat otherwise moribund children. The cost of treatment is 2 Mio $US per patient. Why they started a global lottery early 2020 for 100 babies getting the cure for free, does not seem to carry any inner logic.

# PHARMA'S MARKET

It is good to acknowledge that vocabulary applied played a role in the past and plays one in the present. Many buzzwords are still around and undeletable in corporate language. If ever challenged, semantic mistakes appear to have become part of the DNA of pharmaceutical companies. The only problem yet, using inappropriate terms, lies in the fact that these terms drive thoughts and actions.

The vocabulary used by marketing and salespeople often is derived from the fast-moving consumer goods (FMCG) industry. There were days when senior managers in pharma wanted to hire new product managers from Procter & Gamble and other famous FMCG companies. Pitifully these new colleagues very quickly had been socialized to pharma. "This is all different in pharma and we are not allowed to do this!" were frequently heard sentences. In addition, the question "Who is the customer?" still is unanswered. The metamorphosis from an "ethical drug company" to "customer centricity" therefore could not be achieved.

## Pharma-business in a pseudo-market

In economy there is a clear definition of *market*. Macro-economically, "market" means, to deliberately bring demand and supply together. Searching for "market" Wikipedia talks about *"sellers offering their goods or services (including labor) in exchange for money from buyers"*[7]. Considering these aspects, Coleman's quote from his publication in 1966 "*... the sales-person who never sells to a customer who never buys*" appears to become ever more relevant.

The relevance comes from the mismatch between language and reality: Pharma talks about selling, but no one buys. They use the word customer for people who are not *customers*. Since our language drives thoughts, mind-set and consequently actions, the problem becomes evident in strategies and actions applied and executed. For a number of decades pharma applied FMCG rules to their industry, missing self-reflection. Pharma appears to be resting in itself. The comparison with FMCG-markets though, lets the drug market appear to be more complex indeed. The direct comparison with FMCG-markets clarifies the enormous degree of regulation. If you compare a pharmaceutical market with FMCG-markets, you will see that the word "customer" is inapplicable for a health care provider or prescribing physician.

---

[7] http://en.wikipedia.org/wiki/Market_(economics)

# CHANGES FORCED UPON PHARMA

It is difficult to find a reason why pharma usually waits for changes imposed on them, instead of actively shaping their marketplace or eco-system. Sitting like the rabbit in front of the snake is a widely common practice. There are options and examples how other industries actively challenge their business model and develop it, sometimes they change it themselves in a disruptive way.

## Actively shaping a market – a use-case

If one looks into such a trivial shop like a gas-station, everyone will remember that a gas-station "once upon a time" was a place where you could buy fuel for your car. Sometimes there were people who could give you a hand changing a bulb, add oil or correct tire-pressure for a tip. When margins of petrol became smaller(sic!) and less attractive for the petrol industry, someone must have had the intriguingly innovative idea to transplant the bakery from the other side of the street into the gas-station.

This was a bold move re-shaping a suffering marketplace. Nowadays petrol companies have food and beverage affiliates and more than 80% of the margin of a gas-station is the result of the convenience-shop. The place itself still is called "gas-station". We today use this gas-station as a quite expensive place to shop. But from a customer perspective, higher prices are easily compensated by the degree of convenience offered.

What makes a gas-station a convenience shop?

- Close-by parking any time
- The available product-range is clear and known
- From car to cash it is a few meters only
- It is on your way home
- Shopping and payment are quick and easy

These points are some of the reasons that such a concept helps to significantly improve bottom line. Customer's price sensitivity in the shop is low, whereas it might be considerably higher at the petrol-pump. One could have the impression that, in contrast to the petrol industry, pharma sits and waits until politicians and payers dictate or reshape their business model.

## Reluctance to change

In the past decade about every conference, every writer and most senior managers in pharmaceutical companies shared the news of "change is everywhere". *Change* is yet another buzzword. The term "Change Management" almost reached the quality of a new discipline in management, HR and training. A lot of this change has been imposed on the business-model of the pharmaceutical industry.

For example, no longer are prescribing decisions made by doctors, the majority of blockbuster drugs already lost their exclusivity and are available as generics from many manufacturers.

New compounds or biologicals must prove superiority in outcome before being registered and granted market access or reimbursement. Albeit pharma's mind-set seems to be resting in itself, dating back to a time which is gone. Still pushed aside or even actively neglected, but "all of a sudden" the world around pharma advanced fast in its metamorphosis from the old world. The day when physicians have been the only therapy decision-makers. Today and ever more in the future, the decision-making power of prescribers is marginalizing and, in many countries and product categories lost already.

The stakeholders who decide today, which drug is available or used are different and in most cases are of an institutional nature. There are three categories of decision-making immediately affecting pharma:

1. Decisions about the availability of a drug
2. Decisions about the prescription of a drug
3. Decisions about taking / consuming a drug

To prescribe a drug is possible after it is registered and granted market access. Once availability in a pharmacy, at the chemist next door or the hospital pharmacy is ensured, a prescription can be filled, and the drug being administered.

If diagnosis and labelling match, everything seems to be fine. When a drug is not covered by an insurance or reimbursement scheme, physicians hardly will prescribe it. Prescribing decisions are supported if a drug is insurance covered, recommended by peers, or included in a therapeutic guideline.

If a drug must be paid out-of-pocket, a physician would probably not prescribe, because of the cost-burden he would put on the patient. In this case, the Essential Drug List or any other kind of reimbursement list "decides", if a drug will be prescribed.

A huge proportion of patients, the WHO says 50%, decide to stop taking the drug as prescribed or do not refill their scripts. This highly popular habit is called "non-adherence" and stands for one of the most pressing issues in healthcare. Nowhere in healthcare more money and effort are wasted than with patients who do not take their medication.

## Who does not change, will be changed

In more and more countries, pharma is confronted with the emergence of "real" markets. The demand-side is there and executed and the supply provided by pharma. If it is Medicare or governmental payers, private or public insurers, they pay for drugs. Entities of this kind execute demand.

The demand side has popped up powerfully, playing the market game. They often are believed to say: "We have a demand, we pay, and so you make us happy with low prices!" A whiff of a tragedy lies in the fact that pharma did not show the will or the ability to shape these newly established marketplaces. Pharma developed the role and attitude of complaining about changes being detrimental to their old yet successful business model. Political will was opposed once it became evident. Pharma's most common approach is to lobby against transformation, rejecting change.

Pharma companies often oppose things, especially those that would evidently reduce or jeopardize their revenue, margin or only their comfort zone. In the new ecosystems created, driven, and shaped by political will, being reactive only appears to be the wrong approach. Demography, austerity, patient outcome, and quality of care appear to be keywords in the foreseeable future.

Contrasting suffering healthcare-budgets, pharma companies regularly report huge profits and the amount of money available and invested for mergers and acquisitions is breath-taking.

*"Have you ever heard of a yearly press-conference, where a pharmaceutical company, besides their financial statements, reported about the number of patients treated with their products, the reduction of burden-of-disease, or the degree of improving quality-of-life of their patients?"*

An option for a novel direction has been indicated late April 2020 in a Pharmaphorum interview. Manuel Reiberg, GM of Daiichi Sankyo UK, in 2021 indicated a pathway to design the future. This fully matches the concept of Key Account Management: establishing a fruitful and lasting partnership designed to solve problems in healthcare by delivering value "beyond the pill." Applicable everywhere.

**Pharma needs to become NHS-expert** 8

If pharma wants to help the NHS improve outcomes, it needs to do so through a true partnership rather than a transactional relationship. That's according to Daiichi Sankyo's UK managing director Manuel Reiberg, whose goal is to make sure the firm is a "responsible pharma company".

Reiberg says this approach rests on two pillars: gathering insights and expertise from across the health system to become a provider of "genuine solutions"; and responsibly partnering with the NHS to identify inefficiencies and deliver new, effective, and sustainable healthcare across the UK.

"We need to go beyond just supplying medicines," Reiberg says. "We need to have a way of becoming an integral part of collectively addressing the challenges in our healthcare system. "That means we are looking beyond just selling drugs, and instead understanding how we can support diagnosis, adherence, or even prevention programmes."

One of the first things Reiberg set out to do when he joined the UK arm of Daiichi Sankyo was to better understand the country's healthcare environment and the relationship between pharma and the NHS.

---

8   https://pharmaphorum.com/views-analysis-market-access/daiichi-sankyo-pharma-needs-to-become-nhs-experts/

"It's a very complex, fragmented environment with a lot of devolved decision-making," he says. "I realised very quickly that I couldn't manage the company from the boardroom. We had to find an operating model that devolved our decision-making as close as possible to our customers." (end of excerpt)

# DEFINITIONS & VOCABULARY

The term "Key Account Management" is missing in Wikipedia (early 2020)[9]. In this case it makes a lot of sense to clarify what key account management in its narrow sense should stand for.

> *KAM describes a marketing-methodology designed and executed to establish lasting, fruitful, and robust partnerships between businesses.*

## ENSURE COMMON UNDERSTANDING

The term KAM is frequently used and almost omnipresent in the pharmaceutical industry of today. Have a look at job postings to gain insight about the most various meanings of KAM. In order to achieve a mutual understanding of the whole subject, terms must be clear. Below definitions will be valid whenever any of these appears in this book. You will gain a lot, when the acronym's three letters finally will be clarified and defined in your organisation.

---

[9] The page "KEY ACCOUNT MANAGEMENT" does not exist.
https://en.wikipedia.org/w/index.php?search=KEY+ACCOUNT+MANAGEMENT

## The major letter: A for Account

> *An account is an entity, institution, or network in which the decision-making about registration, listing, reimbursement, purchasing, usage, or recommendation of a product or service involves a number of people.*

### The first letter: K for Key

A very small number of accounts, a fraction to be specified, are KEY for your organisation. Only to these few a dedicated KEY person, a Key Account Manager will be assigned to. All other places to which the definition applies are called accounts. The "K" will be missing, so will be a dedicated Key Account Manager.

### The third letter: M for Management

The Key Account Manager manages the internal KAM-team, consisting of multiple subject-matter experts, necessary to best possibly serve the KEY Account in an endeavour to establish a lasting and robust business-to-business relationship.

# Key Account

> *Key are those accounts, which are of top / key priority and relevance for a specific objective or the company as a whole.*

It is of major importance to understand, that only few accounts are and should be called **key**. Non-Key-Accounts simply are called and treated as *accounts*. Further down, we will share with you how to identify those accounts and which rules and procedures could be applied.

## Account potential

The word potential usually needs a prefix to clarify its meaning. In Human Resources potential is something very different from sales and marketing. *Account-potential* needs careful description and definition as well.

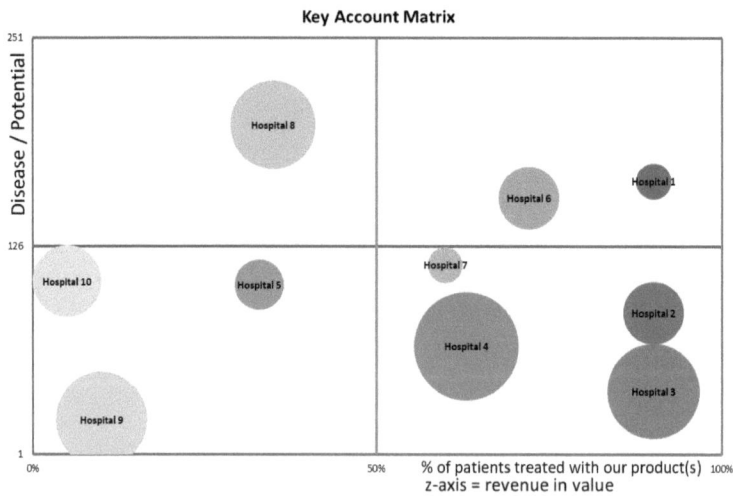

**EXHIBIT 5: SAMPLE MATRIX**

In all regularity the word *potential* is a figure used for calculations. This is why *potential* must have a definition, feasible for calculation and statistics. As you can see in our descriptive matrix example, potential is indicated on the y-axis. It is an almost global habit that the y-axis stands for something which lies beyond your company's reach, whereas the x-axis indicates a parameter lying within the immediate reach of your company's influence.

This is how *potential* may be defined:

$$Potential = \frac{market\ size}{weighted\ (100 - x)} * \frac{market\ growth}{weighted\ 100\ (100 - x)}$$

The rationale for this definition is that it is applicable across the universe. You can e.g., calculate the market-potential of continents, country groups, countries, territories, and even drill down to a single hospital, physician, or pharmacist with exactly the same equation. No assumptions, no guesses. This *potential* is a numerical fact. If you only want to refer to the market size when calculating, there is no reason to use any other term than the term *market size*? This is the most appropriate way to resolve regular misunderstandings of *potential*.

It still fascinates how many different meanings, connotations, and perceptions are available around the word *potential*. Remember: *"There can only be one!"*

Using different words for the same subject is misleading your colleagues' thoughts and causes relevant losses in working-efficiency, due to inconsistencies in understanding.

### Decision Making Unit (DMU)

By nature of an account, there is a "number of people" involved in making decisions. These individuals involved, are members of the "decision making unit". [10]

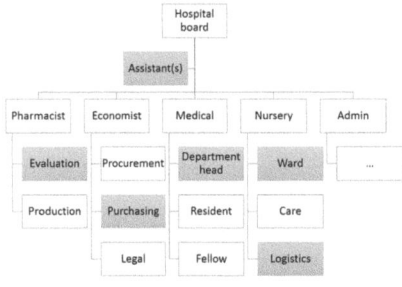

**EXHIBIT 6: ORG-CHART EXAMPLE**

The Decision-Making-Unit is a network of people. It does show both formal and informal aspects. The very first step is to find or collect the organization chart of an account and highlight those who are, by their function, involved in making decisions.

### *Management* in KAM

It must be clear that it does not make sense to assume that a key account manager *"manages an account"*.

> Example:
> Your company may even be a key account for some of your providers. But if it is IQVIA® or SalesForce® or apple®: none of them manages you or even your company.

The "M" in KAM stands for managing the necessary and normal internal KAM-Team.

Rationale for the KAM Team: An individual Key Account Manager cannot meet all needs and demands of all DMU-members by himself. He needs colleagues, subject-matter experts, supporting the complex and manifold tasks when establishing a robust, fruitful, and lasting business relationship. Identifying the necessary skills and

---

[10] The term "buying centre" is synonymous

competencies, forming, briefing, and guiding a team in the KAM-process, undoubtedly needs managerial skills.

## Needs and wants

Much is said about needs and need-orientation. What often is missing is to clarify what a "need" is. The word *need* is another, apparently sloppily used word in the language of pharma business. Philip Kotler distinguishes between the more "psychological" needs and rather "factual" wants / demands.

*A human need is a state of deprivation of some basic satisfaction. People require food, clothing, shelter, safety, belonging, and esteem. These needs are not created by society or by marketers. They exist in the very texture of human biology and the human condition. Wants are desires for specific satisfiers of needs. Although people's needs are few, their wants are many.* (Kotler, 2008)

Referring to the institutional business in KAM, the word "need" is used in its psychological context, related to the five steps in Maslow's "pyramid of needs". The word "wants" indicates more factual wants, demands, requirements, or necessities to improve the delivery of healthcare.

## Strategy

Strategy is a word frequently used, sounding important, carrying a connotation of something lasting or reaching into the future. The proper understanding and the resulting usage of the term "strategy" will save time supporting people's understanding and improve working efficiency.

There is a "managerial triple-jump" consisting of objective, then strategy[11], followed by actions or tactics.

"Strategos" is the Greek word for the highest-ranking military commander. The word "strategy" itself and all those discussions and strategy tools are derived and connected with the "art of war".[12]

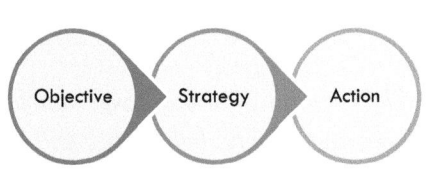

**EXHIBIT 7: MANAGERIAL TRIPLE JUMP**

Etymology of *Strategy*: By nature of the role, a military commander (GR: strategos) sets the objective like: "We must cross this river!"

His "direct reports", leaders of the different branches of arms, will have to find answers to the question: "<u>How</u> can we cross this river?" Once they made their decisions, each will report or share their suggestions with their commander.

*Strategos* will then finally decide, how his army will proceed in the pursuit of achieving the given goal. *Strategy* therefore can be defined as the answer to the question "**How** will we achieve the objective?" Only after a strategic decision has been made and the way forward is clear, the preparation of tactics will be released, and subsequent actions executed. When this sequence is strictly followed and complied with, success and the underlying strategy will be dependent on each other.

---

[11] "On War", Carl von Clausewitz, (1780–1831)
[12] *"The Art of War"* (孫子兵法) is a Chinese thesis by Sun Tzu (500 BC).

## Performance – the "unknown creature"

Our industry is flooded with consultants who keep talking about benchmarks and best practices trying to establish high performing companies with high performance people. The problem is: *Performance is an Unknown Creature.* (Wolfram, Hanno, 2014)

You may have heard a reporter commenting a match like this:

*"The team showed a great performance, but pitifully lost!"*
Only a week later the same reporter says:
*"The team showed a great performance and won."*

Managers at every level talk about your, their, the company's and other's *performance*. Often you can hear them talk about high-performing teams and low-performing reps. The core question is what they mean with this word? Often it is used to even start or justify usually premature managerial consequences. So far, a valid and binding definition of *performance* appears to be missing in the business context.

To describe a clear and calculable value indicating performance with the same metric(s) across a specific group of people is needed. Please be clear that if a manager means good results, then the word *result* should be used. If someone talks about working long hours every day, you call this "input" or "effort". Below "definition-attempt" could serve as a first attempt.

> *"Performance is a value to calculate an index made-up of specific metrics of input and output or effort and result."*

## Communication

Due to frequent misunderstandings and many managers complaining about people not having understood what they *"have so clearly communicated with already three email blasts"*, it appears to be necessary to clarify what *communication* means and how the term should be used and understood.

*Communication* in its narrow sense is a social act, involving people, exchanging, interacting, sending and receiving, encoding and decoding messages. Admittedly, gestures facial expression, body language and the tonality of speech are associated aspects of inter-human communication. Only the combination of all these facets establishes communication in the true sense of the word.

A phone call is already missing some aspects of "real" communication. Although words and the tonality of speech are there, gestures and facial expressions we only extrapolate from what we hear. Painful, far-reaching, and disconnecting misunderstandings and misinterpretations happen caused by insufficient communication.

Remember:

---

*Interpersonal communication is not about **saying** something.*
*We communicate to **cause** something.*

---

Therefore, we should re-consider using the word "communication" for writing e-mails, texting, using messenger services, or any other kind of electronically transmitted / written messages. WhatsApp® messages are as far away from communication as Facebook-**friends** are real friends. Using electronic tools, fails to meet the basic requirements of communication being a "social act". Electronic transmissions carry truncated *communication* and are used to *inform* each other.

A serious indicator that you are no longer communicating in the narrow sense of the word is starting or wanting to use emoticons. ☺

Emojis follow an important rationale when being used: the writer tries to make sure that the receiver perceives the message with similar emotions as the sender had them typing the message. Managers trying to "communicate" with their people through e-mail will regularly fail. Information or sharing documents and dates: great. Communication: hardly. Electronic media are great for transmitting information in a simple and efficient way.

Interpersonal communication, face2face, stands for unreplaceable human interaction. This is, by the way, the most important justification that a human being is the by far the best and most efficient interface between enterprises and market participants, customers, and stakeholders.

The boom of videoconferencing during the Covid-19 pandemic, shows exactly this. Talking face-to-face through video is the option closest to interhuman communication in the narrow sense.

## KAM live

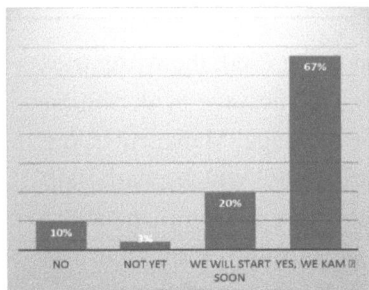

EXHIBIT 8: POLLING RESULT,
n=50

*The acronym KAM itself is used almost everywhere, meaning something different to almost everyone.*

Already in 2010, the Cegedim Dendrite Market Access[13] report found that 83% of all pharmaceutical companies have Key Account Management implemented. This allows the hypothesis that in the majority of companies, Key Account Management only shows marginal differences against the "hospital sales force". Even senior managers admit that KAM in their case stands for a renamed yet traditional hospital business.

Early 2014 we did a brief check on the same subject at a conference in Warsaw, Poland. The question was: *"Do you employ Key Account Managers?"* 67% of senior managers participating said: "Yes, we have key account managers." Once asked for more detail, most of them admitted that they meant their hospital field force. Applying the acronym KAM sounded more fashionable and was appreciated by their employees.

Being a "Key Account Manager" sounds better than being a hospital rep or a hospital specialist.

---

13

https://www.cegedim.com/communique/Cegedim%20Dendrite_MarketAccessReport_08062010_eng.pdf

## Customer or account

Preparing the predecessor of this book dedicated to the German Market, we researched the understanding of what an account is and how to define "account". To some degree and driven by experience, we expected the outcome of this research. It still was surprising: Many (68% of respondents) believed that an "account" is the same as or a synonym for "customer". Wrong!

| Customer | Account |
|---|---|
| An individual | An entity, enterprise, network, or group of people |
| Decides by him- or herself | Many people contribute and play a role in decision-making |
| "One that purchases a commodity, service or right."[14] | An organisation orders and acquires a product, service, or right. |

Quite some time has passed since the German textbook on Key Account Management had been published, many discussions with bright, experienced people in the pharmaceutical industry have happened, and a decent number of consulting projects delivered since then.

A reasonable number of keynotes and conferences later, the definition of "account" still appears to be volatile. It cannot be repeated often enough: having a common and mutual understanding of terms is crucial to any organisation. This leads to enormous communicational frictions, a waste of time, misunderstandings, and prolonged meetings delivering little to no outcome or value.

---

[14] https://www.merriam-webster.com/dictionary/customer

Asking people what an *account* is, very normally leads to a number of examples, seldom if at all, to a definition. The vast majority of answers indicate that a hospital or a group of hospitals are accounts. These answers undoubtedly are true in most cases, but an example hardly defines something.

## ACCOUNT-VARIATIONS

We conducted a survey reaching out to 11 countries receiving answers from 16 senior managers in the pharmaceutical industry. The open question was "What is an account?" The answers have been quite startling, and experience shows that today the degree of variation appears to be the same. Below is an excerpt of the astonishing list of answers to the question: **"What is an Account?"**

- *Relationship with all sort of organizations...*
- *An account is an individual or a group of individuals who take a common and unique decision for a specific issue. These individuals will have different profiles (both personal and professional) and might interact to reach an agreement.*
- *An account is a sales/business term to describe an established book of business.*
- *Typically, an account is synonymous with a specific client company, example: in Pharma, a wholesaler could be an account, a specific hospital would be an account, a chain of pharmacies could be an account.*
- *An account is every institution/person which/who can contribute to your turnover and/or profit. Every entity able to purchase the services/products you sell.*
- *Being an account means building a relationship between buyer and seller.*
- *(Potential) Customer, group, KOL, etc. which (may) need my services, goods etc, or may prove beneficial for the company in other ways (e.g. KOL, networking, ...).*

- *An account is a number of people, who mutually agree on the usage / purchase or introduction of a product or service within a business.*
- *Customer*
- *An account is not a client, a prescriber, etc. An account is not a single person. Above all, an account has to be conceived as an organization that is a complex system consisting of decisions. So, an account is not a bigger client, it is something completely different.*
- *Account is a "unit; place" where the business relevant decision is influenced by more stakeholders. The location of a group of customers who have authority to influence the market outcome for our products.*
- *Account = customer who produce profit or have the potential to do. In fact, that is the target company. In our business an account is a company (group of individuals).*
- *Client or prospect that can generate, directly or indirectly, revenue for my business.*
- *A financial relationship between two companies in which an account would be a customer, usually purchasing a range of products/services from the company could be a hospital, a purchasing authority or a pharmacy chain.*
- *A customer who is not making decisions him or herself, but in a DMU.* [Decision Making Unit]

**Customer** is one of the most carelessly used words in the pharmaceutical industry. One must fully be aware of the risks of such careless usage. It does cause a lot of harm, misunderstandings, creates weird connotations, and drives company strategies and actions towards unwanted directions. In many pharma companies, everyone of interest nowadays seems to be called "customer". In some companies, this word is even applied to colleagues next door. They are called "internal customers". This development appears to cause tragic mistakes and aberrations.

*Customer centricity* is prevalent in many speeches and projects. Using the word "customer" negligently for people who are not and probably never will be a "customer" to a pharmaceutical company, causes many misunderstandings and people can get lost, when it comes to strategy execution.

---

*Knowing and using correct terms in their correct context is a vital prerequisite for the coherent execution of strategy.*

---

### CUSTOMER: A DEFINITION

The economic definition of the word "customer" is straightforward and clear: *A customer is an **Individual** who **has bought** a product or service.* Taking this definition as given, a prescribing physician never was, is or will be a customer in this sense of the word. Using "customer" for anyone who might be a target, or a stakeholder dilutes meaning and importance of the word and misdirects mind-set and actions.

Business economics tell us that there are several steps before someone converts to be a *customer*:

1. Suspect =    could become a customer
2. Prospect =   will probably become a customer
3. Customer =   has bought a good, service, or right

**Note:**
The word "customer" does not apply to a medical doctor in the role as a prescriber, user, or recommender of a drug. This is especially important for field forces, since words like *negotiating*, and *closing a deal* can never mean the same with prescribers as in a transactional

business setting. In this book, we will carefully stick to definitions and will apply the word "customer" only when applicable.

## Transactional business

Whenever a pharmaceutical salesforce is visiting prescribing physicians, there is no buyer, let alone a customer. Transactions do not happen and what the sales- force does is everything but *selling*.

Account Management is different: It is about demand and supply, it is about bringing offerings and purchasing together and at the end, there is cash for product, service or right. In an account-management setting, products, services, or rights are exchanged against money.

Account Management in its essence, and different from traditional field-forces, is a transactional business.

# PHARMA'S STAKEHOLDERS

Political decisions have created a true healthcare **market** in the narrow sense of economy. Lawmakers have established a "demand-side" in healthcare. The demand-side is deliberately paired with pharma as the supplier.

In addition to the demand-side, payers, governments, legal bodies, other entities, or authorities have been established and granted far reaching decision-making power.

Each of these entities, except the patient, is an **account**. Depending on your company and portfolio, any could be decided and selected as **key** account.

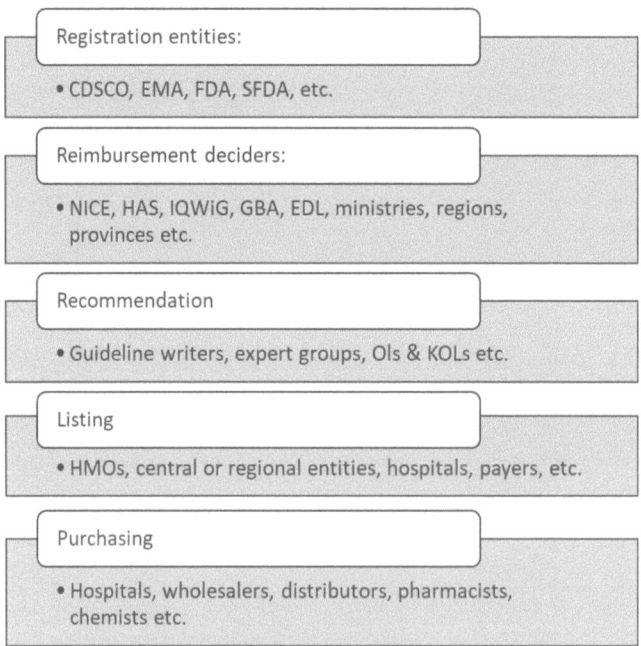

Registration entities:

• CDSCO, EMA, FDA, SFDA, etc.

Reimbursement deciders:

• NICE, HAS, IQWiG, GBA, EDL, ministries, regions, provinces etc.

Recommendation

• Guideline writers, expert groups, Ols & KOLs etc.

Listing

• HMOs, central or regional entities, hospitals, payers, etc.

Purchasing

• Hospitals, wholesalers, distributors, pharmacists, chemists etc.

**EXHIBIT 9: MARKET ACCESS STAKEHOLDERS**

# REGISTRATION

Entities or institutions like the **China Food and Drug Administration** (CFDA), today called National Medical Products Administration (NMPA), the **Food and Drug Administration** in the United States (FDA), the **Central Drugs Standard Control Organization** (CDSCO) in India, or the **European Medicines Agency** (EMA) decide about a product's marketing authorisation. As a lowest common denominator, the task of all these entities is to register a product and include it in the respective national registry of drugs or devices.

These regulatory agencies overlook manufacturing, trade and certain aspects of marketing. Their common task is being a watchdog, making sure that the promises made by the pharmaceutical industry are correct, and product claims are supported by reliable and valid research results. Drug safety is another major concern, as are many topics around pharmacovigilance. Each of these entities must be known, respected, and treated as an important stakeholder in the market. They constitute high-ranking decision-making bodies in today's world of healthcare. Making their role even more significant lies in the mostly binary nature of their decisions. It is about *On* or *Off*, *in* or *out* of the market. For many pharmaceutical companies, these institutions top the list of Key Accounts for the pharmaceutical industry.

# PRICING AND REIMBURSEMENT

Another major prerequisite to successfully market a pharmaceutical product is gaining reimbursement status. This status about the degree of reimbursement varies by healthcare-system. There are drugs or devices being fully reimbursed. This means patients are treated for free. In some countries essential drug-lists or national reimbursement lists exist. Drugs or devices may be part of free access to healthcare as promised to citizens. Reimbursed only to a certain percentage or a flat fee per prescription to be paid by the patient are alternatives in some countries. There are countries where the price granted depends on variable aspects. A more and more common way to compare and set a price for reimbursement is establishing a price basket. In this case, the average-price in a specific set of countries plays a role as "reference price".

A pretty unexpected presidential order has been signed by the President of the United States in September 2020[15]. It requests Medicare to pay the same price for certain expensive prescription drugs that other countries do. It is called the "most-favoured-nation price."

This will leave pharma unable to argue for a higher price in the US as it was possible in the past. Incoherent pricing will backfire on pricing policies of pharma, missing coherence and lacking consistency across countries. The days of national solo-pricing attempts in pricing evidently are gone.

Missing the precious reimbursement status, can be a reason to withdraw an application for a specific drug or device from the respective market. A number of Biosimilars have fallen victim to this already. Another common denominator of "pricing and reimbursement"-entities is, that many have started a closer look at a novel drug's added value or additional therapeutic benefit. The requested price is compared to the current standard therapy. A new drug no longer is welcome only because it is new. NCEs or biological medicines are carefully examined and evaluated to which degree they deliver better outcome for patients than the current therapeutic regimen. Most evaluating bodies deciding about reimbursement, usually work in a transparent and professional way. Although regions or provinces may have different ideas and concepts. Consequently, the

---

[15] https://edition.cnn.com/2020/09/13/politics/trump-drug-prices-executive-order/index.html

results for reimbursement can be different. Reimbursement "yes" or "no" is one part of the game. If you ever are caught by surprise, your Key Account Management is not working properly.

Patient outcome is one side of the coin and cost is the other. Like in some other markets the *total cost of treatment*[16] is gaining weight as a central threshold to reimbursement. Similar to "total cost of ownership" of industrial goods, this metric can display a moment of truth. Scientific "health benefit data could well be a threat to novel treatment options.

> "Additionally, three health technology assessment (HTA) organizations are collaborating on how to adapt their cost-effectiveness and value for money assessments. The US-based Institute for Clinical and Economic Review (ICER), England's National Institute for Health and Care Excellence and the Canadian Agency for Drugs and Technologies in Health (CADTH) are to work together on the *valuing a cure project*."[17] The current hype around big data will distil itself playing a major role identifying the "TCO" or "Total Cost of Treatment" in real life. Big data will allow to reveal the full range of healthcare cost like medication + hospital + procedure + outpatient visits + concomitant medication + missing at labour + social cost etc. Ethical values play a role as well."

Remember Novartis' pricing of Zolgensma®. It is a gene-therapy used to treat children younger than 2 years with spinal muscular atrophy (SMA) at a cost of 2 million US$. Ethical questions lie on both sides: authorities will have to decide if access to this treatment can be denied

---

[16] "Total cost of ownership." (TCO)
[17] Pharmaceutical Market Europe, February 2019, www.PMLive.com

to those in need because of its price. The manufacturer must decide if the price must be this high and if shareholder value is the ultimate goal.

# RECOMMENDATION OF A THERAPY

The inclusion of a drug, a medical device, or digital therapeutics into a set of therapeutic guidelines may be similarly prerequisite for success. At minimum, recommendations will be an advantage for the commercialization of a drug. In the era of evidence-based medicine, the outspoken recommendation by experts becomes more relevant than ever. Stakeholders relevant for the recommendation of a drug or device are people contributing to, suggesting, and involved in "making" therapeutic guidelines.

Expert groups in medical centres or medical schools specialized around a specific disease, are actively involved in setting the scene for the therapy of choice. When it comes to orphan diseases and their treatment, cooperation of experts is mandatory. In this context the usage of the fancy and fashionable three-letter acronym "KOL" stands out. Admittedly, there are plenty of variations of so-called Key Opinion Leaders. Only few are really KEY. However, the remarkable detail and smallest common denominator around KOLs is, that all of them are members of groups and teams, never alone and by themselves. Thought-leading and other outstanding people in medicine are always part of a network of subject matter experts.

*A singular person might be the voice, but whatever opinion-leading message is stated, it originates from the work, expertise, and influence of many.*

Being part of a recommended therapeutic regimen, will establish market access in the true sense of the word.

# LISTING

Another step on the pathway to market is listing a product or device. "Listing" is the act of putting a drug or device into the "list of treatment options" inside a specific healthcare providing entity or organisation.

No HMO (health maintenance organization) or PBM (Pharmaceutical Benefit Manager) and most other payor-organizations, will allow their contractual physicians or nurses to simply prescribe whatever is available or individuals believe makes sense.

The judgment about a therapy to be suggested or prescribed or the therapeutic freedom of individual prescribers is limited. The decision-making power of an individual doctor ends when a product is missing on the respective drug list.

Listing in organizations like an HMO or hospital depends on several aspects, which need to be covered by a pharmaceutical company and their Key Account Managers. Listing happens after successful negotiations with a drug committee usually to be found as members of a formal network inside the respective entity.

Before an entity has not approved a product to be listed, registration, reimbursement, and even being part of a guideline, will not suffice to create revenue or grant patients access to this specific treatment option.

# PURCHASING

Many have encountered the experience that a registered and reimbursed product is on a list but not ordered or re-ordered.

Hospitals, wholesalers, distributors, pharmacists, and chemists who order a product, might have their own agenda. Along the distribution chain, across a country or inside a hospital, more influencers than expected show to have a voice.

There might be individuals or groups in departments or elsewhere, making many efforts of no earthly use.

A quite evident example is the generic's market of today, where many companies compete in the market with the same INN. Having a product listed by no means is a guarantee for revenue. Even receiving an order followed by the delivery of a drug only is a first step towards revenue for a pharmaceutical company. Ordering needs repetition.

Key Account Managers will have to carefully follow-up, what happens with a product once it is made available inside a hospital.

# MORE INFLUENCE(R)S

There are several obstacles to be surmounted before a pharmaceutical product creates revenue and gets the chance to pay back its research and development cost. The five categories (see exhibit above) or groups of stakeholders are not all new species. Some of them are in the scope of the pharmaceutical industry already.

The issue is that companies need to deal with all of them in a coherent[18] and consistent[19] manner. The fact that everything and everyone today is globally interconnected by digital means, establishes full transparency if you want it or not. *Digital* means as well that every person in each of these entities in any country can interact with each other easily.

Most prominent items for global interactions are market access, indication areas, the results of pricing negotiations, or reimbursement rules in a single market. All details are globally available for comparison. No matter if it is leaked information or deliberately made available for the interested public. This justifies the urgent requirement that the pharmaceutical industry hast structures in place which allow full transparency, coherence, and consistency across all their touchpoints, even across different countries or continents. To ensure exactly this, some industries employ Global Key Account Managers. Ask Siemens or Huawei or IQVIA if they appear closer to you.

Pharmaceutical companies usually are fairly good at identifying their stakeholders. The systemic problem built in organisational structures: is the question: "who the heck is in charge and responsible for each of these touchpoints?" The discussion often ends in lengthy disputes

---

[18] systematic or logical connection – www.merriam-webster.com/dictionary
[19] In classical deductive logic, a consistent theory is one that does not entail a contradiction. https://en.wikipedia.org/wiki/Consistency

between departments. Market-access, launch-readiness, medical, medical-liaison, marketing, or hospital sales are the most evident departments fighting for or denying ownership. Each of them wants to be in charge. At this early point of the allocation of stakeholders, company-wide coherence and consistency are at risk. Department heads follow department-individual objectives, and need to meet their internal metrics, while executing remarkably "different business-models".

In this context we need to remember and consider that the word "department" by its origin, is derived from "*to depart*" in the sense of to *withdraw*. The term *department* carries a connotation of separation and often drives a mindset of walls between them. *Department* usually stands for, causes and conservation of siloed mentality and approaches.

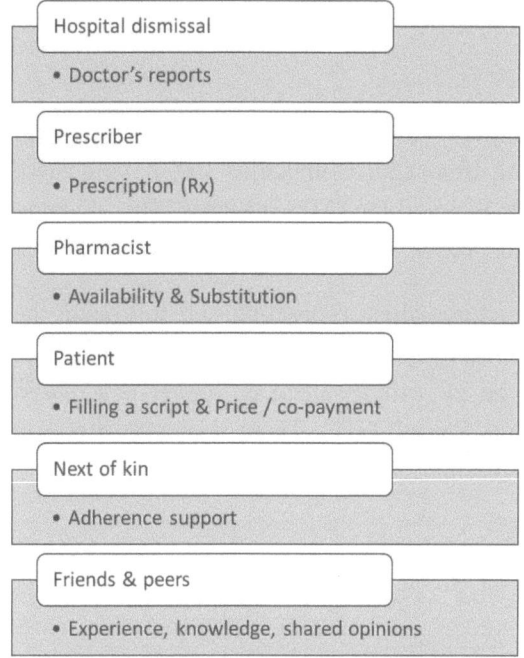

These six touchpoints must be considered by pharma or medtech as well, since any of these is equipped with an **on-off-switch** for pharma's revenue streams.

Any of these individuals (= not an account and not even *customers*) can prevent pay-back of pharma's research and development cost and intervene with the success of key account managers.

**EXHIBIT 10: TOUCH-POINTS, CONTINUED**

# Rx / OTC-SEPARATION: A WEAKNESS

A majority of pharmaceutical companies perpetuates a structural problem established a long time ago: Companies still have a stark dividing line between their Rx- and the OTC-business. This division between Rx and OTC establishes walls between distribution channels.

If pharma keeps these structures alive, respecting and following the much-promised patient's journey cannot happen. In the complex age of healthcare-delivery in the 21$^{st}$ century there no longer is a reason separating the business-units Rx and OTC. There is plenty of reason and rationale to end this artificial line of separation.

*The tradition of separating OTC- and Rx-business can be blamed for the inability of pharma to become patient centric.*

In earlier days, this separation might have carried a rationale from the producer's perspective. It followed the logic of the assumed different distribution channels of the past:

- In the old and paternalistic days of care, the prescribing physician was the only decision maker. With the script he ultimately decided which drug was right and to be taken by the patient.
- The pharmacist had to dispense the product as prescribed. Substitution was legally forbidden and prosecuted.
- The field of OTC, non-prescription, over-the-counter drugs, fully was the pharmacist's domain. Consequently, the industry established separate business units. They executed their promotional and selling endeavours towards pharmacists

and did not allow interference by Rx-division, let alone cooperation between their field forces.

Looking at these habits from the patient's perspective draws a different picture:

When a patient encounters a health problem, starting with minor importance, he will ask the pharmacist to recommend a remedy. When a patient already has an idea about the cure of choice himself, he will directly ask the pharmacist for a brand classified as Non-Rx.

# EXCURSION: PHARMACY

The term "patient journey" is frequently used, heard, and talked about. Is it lip service only or does the pharmaceutical industry mean it? Let us have a brief glimpse at the patient journey.

Patient's health problems sometimes last and exacerbate. "Headache" may turn into migraine, and a dripping nose can be an allergy moving to lower airways causing asthma. Simple coughs over time may develop into a serious COPD.

One day, the responsible pharmacist will suggest consulting a physician. Many patients themselves will extend their search for a solution by themselves and much later seek advice from a physician.

# A patient journey

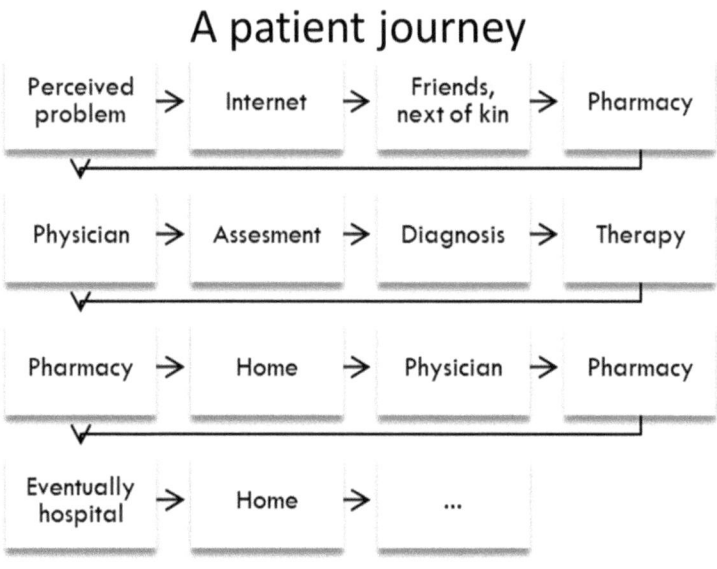

**EXHIBIT 11: THE PATIENT JOURNEY**

Once a diagnosis is established and a drug prescribed, this will again bring the patient back to his pharmacist. The loop of any patient journey is then closed and ready for regular repetition. Do pharmacists not deserve much more attention and serious considerations in the marketing-efforts of Rx-pharma? In a world full of INNs, legal frameworks encourage or even force the pharmacist to select the drug to be dispensed. Should this not drive the industry to seriously reconsider their current Rx/OTC-structure? In all those countries where generic (INN) prescription is standard, the pharmacist is the one deciding which producer's drug will be dispensed to the patient. Imagine a script with Amlodipin 10mg presented at the pharmacy. Who decides which of the Amlodipin-manufacturers will benefit?

In addition, pharmacists play a major role around therapy adherence. They do have an underestimated influence on their customers, usually called patients. In many cases members of the Rx-pharma business-units do not even know pharmacists, let alone are strategies in place to actively integrate pharmacists into the delivery of healthcare.

More and more countries allow pharmacy chains, serving millions of patients. These may well be **Key Accounts** for generic companies and must become action-points for Key Account Management.

Remember: a singular pharmacy or pharmacist rarely is an account. A pharmacy-group or pharmacy-chain for some companies may even be a Key Account.

# PRESCRIPTION AND USAGE

Most stakeholders around the prescription or usage of a product are well known. Prescribing physicians have been the core target group at all times. Some stakeholders for prescription or usage are newer or have not been recognized or cared for by the pharmaceutical industry in the past.

Today we know that nurses play an important role as well. They will of course feedback the handling of syringes, the ease of intake by a hospital patient, or the taste of a drug to their peers and others involved in caring for patients. In some countries, "prescribing nurses" and "physician assistants" are the ones to sign repetitive prescriptions. In most markets, nurses are at least preparing the script. They hand it over, brief the patient, and receive their feedback.

Conclusion: Assistants are important touchpoints for the pharmaceutical industry.

# NEGLECTED DECIDER: PATIENT

According to research from Cap Gemini (Forissier & Katrina Firlik, 2014) *"... revenue loss is estimated to be $564 billion, or 59% of the $956 billion in total global pharmaceutical revenue in 2011."* Only in the United Sates, the revenue lost for the pharmaceutical industry is estimated at 188 billion US$ per year. In principle the "revenue lost" is only one side of the coin. If it is true that around 50% of all patients decide to discontinue drug- therapy, the alarming part is that around the same 50% of all efforts of the healthcare system are in vain, lost and must be written off.

Non-adherent patients hardly can benefit from therapy[20]. Non-adherence affects the whole delivery chain of care negatively. Every minute of work, any effort to find the right diagnose with the intention to treat the problem, is invested e.g. to prevent stroke or myocardial infarction as key risks. They are major exacerbations, or dangerous consequences from untreated elevated blood-pressure. If more than half of all patients do not take their drugs and fail to follow directions given by the doctor or the nurse, the intended prevention cannot happen.

Under such circumstances, drug and any other therapy will fail to deliver the planned result. Drugs cannot achieve what they promised in clinical trials. Since most studies speak about secondary adherence, even the money spent for the first pack of drugs must be written off the healthcare balance sheet.

In the Capgemini (Capgemini Consulting, 2012) report you can read that *"Medication non-adherence is responsible for $290 billion in otherwise avoidable medical spending in the US alone each year"*.

To more powerfully illustrate the matter, IMS Institute for Healthcare Informatics (IMS-Institute, 2012) finds that there are six central inefficiencies in healthcare: "… patient non-adherence, untimely medicine use, antibiotic misuse and overuse, medication errors, suboptimal generic use, and mismanaged polypharmacy…."

Imagine the impact a pharmaceutical or medtech company could have improving health? The benefit for governments, payers, hospitals, caregivers and singular patients, when Pharma and its Key Account Managers would take the chance to move from pushing drugs to solving problems in healthcare, could be huge. Getting actively

---

[20] https://www.who.int/chp/knowledge/publications/adherence_report/en/

involved in the provision of healthcare is what Key Account Management in Pharma means and sh(c)ould stand for.

*Key Account Management is the pharmaceutical's industry door opener to play an active role in healthcare.*

# KEY ACCOUNT MANAGEMENT: THE EAGLE'S VIEW

Although the difference between **Key** **Account Management** and **Account Management,** (without "Key") is remarkable, we will pay tribute to the regular, sloppy usage of the term *Key Account Management* and its three-letter acronym (TLA) *KAM.*

The flow shows the steps needed to establish and execute Key Account Management.

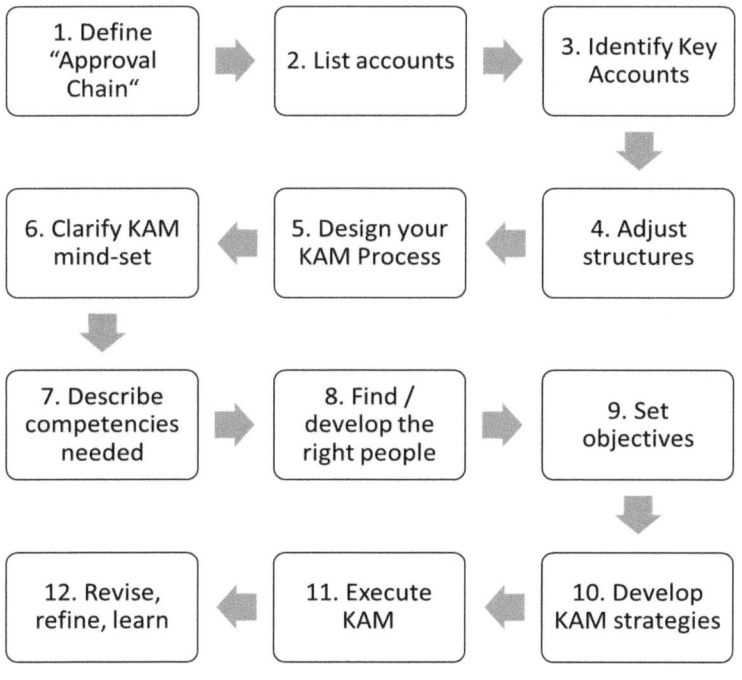

EXHIBIT 12: HOW TO "KAM"

In this early stage, an important *caveat* needs to be raised when it comes to so-called *best practices*. Consulting firms design their projects like a product: ready to use, easily to be multiplied and reproduced.

It is a wise idea to actively avoid *best practices* to be "copy/pasted" from any other company deck into your own organisation. Trying to remain unique is a much better approach. Your procedures, your expertise, your people, and your skills will make the difference in the marketplace. Remember, that there only is one CocaCola, one McDonalds, and one Ikea in this world, despite many attempts to copy.

Competitive advantage and meeting the company's business figures will work if you develop and keep details proprietary and specific to your company.

*Any "one size fits all-approach" will fail.*

The necessity of different approaches toward KAM gets very clear when thinking about the differences between biotech, research-based pharma, marketing a new NCE, marketing an orphan drug or introducing Key Account Management in a generic drugs's setting. The flow of steps may well remain similar. Although the approval chain will vary. The individual company's content will pave the ground for competitive advantage, differentiation, and open ample room to deliver a specific and proprietary footprint in the market.

# KAM - OVERVIEW

In Key Account Management there is one pivotal presumption: organisations, legal bodies, organisations, KOL-networks, and any other kind of decision-making entities are **accounts**. All these are accounts by their nature, existing of "a number of people involved in decision making". Hence business methodologies and procedures like Key Account Management will similarly apply.

Remember the definition of *account*:

*An account is an entity, institution, or network in which the decision-making about registration, listing, reimbursement, purchasing, usage, or recommendation of a product or service involves a number of people.*

Any individual working in an account and being part of the "decision making unit" you may call "stakeholder", "client", "DMU-member" or "*target*".

As stated earlier, the most common, yet wrong word applied is *customer*[21]. Using the term *customer* is inappropriate and wrong in this context. In complex *accounts* customers in the narrow, economic sense of the word are inexistent. Applying the word will deflect people, mindset, and actions.

Remember the definition of the term *customer*:

*One that **purchases** a commodity or service*[22]

---

[21] https://en.wikipedia.org/wiki/Customer
[22] https://www.merriam-webster.com/dictionary/customer

# 1. THE "APPROVAL CHAIN"

Pharmaceutical companies tend to complain about so many restricting regulations. Some of the regulatory rules indeed are specific and do not apply elsewhere. The number of necessary or suggested *approvals* therefore are plenty. Depending on the involved product or portfolio of products, stakeholders along the "approval chain" vary. By nature of account management, all stakeholders are members of a group or team. At all approval steps, the definition of account, being a multitude of people contributing to decisions, remains valid. Listing every single instance or approving authority related to your offering or portfolio in the respective market is a vitally important first step.

# 2. FIND AND LIST ALL ACCOUNTS

Collecting entities along and around the approval chain, shows one major issue: you need them all. Any entity you miss at this early stage, will vanish from your radar. Once not on your list, the respective entity will be out of focus for a long time. The risk is missing an important chain-link along the approval and marketing process. Once the list is completed, you will have a valuable list of *accounts* in your country. The list may look differently for other companies. It is a wise idea to use your own skills and expertise to determine and compile this comprehensive list.

# 3. IDENTIFY YOUR KEY ACCOUNTS

In terms of setting up and documenting(!) the internal identification-process of key accounts, it is a must to suggest, decide and carefully lay down *why* which accounts are defined or set as KEY for your organisation. The top 5% or 10% of accounts showing the highest importance for market access, the most relevant decision-making power, the highest, number of patients, or market size, may be ennobled to be your KEY accounts. Depending on your business setting there may easily be other valid criteria.

As an example of what can be meant with varying and different criteria to identify KEY accounts, have a look at Zolgensma®.

This treatment option by Novartis® is offered at a cost of around US$ 2 million per child cured from an otherwise fatal disease. Market authorisation is not a problem at all. In such a case, any entity approving cost or price is of utmost importance or KEY. National committees on medicinal ethics will have to be considered, just as the "public" and "published opinion". Payer-organizations and reimbursement deciders will most probably be categorized as KEY accounts.

## 4. ADJUST YOUR STRUCTURES

KAM lives on and needs "cross-functional collaboration". Most probably a buzzword must be actively brought to life. Mapping all internal units, functions and people that may need to cooperate is the next step.

Key Account Management deals with your most important accounts. Internal support will be necessary and needed from across the organisation. When carefully checking current structures, you will be able to identify or anticipate obstructions and barriers conflicting with the introduction of comprehensive collaboration. KAM needs a specific structure, enabling seamless, agile, and cross-functional cooperation. It is a wise idea to design and determine your own, proprietary, unique, and future proof organisational structure.

# 5. DESIGN A KAM PROCESS

It is a wise idea to design the optimal process for your company, following your new structure to reduce frictions and foreseeable delays when dealing with your key accounts.

Later in this book we shall drill further into detail of a sample KAM process. Be aware that the book serves as guidance and food for thought. It is not written as a cookbook, applying to all and everything. It may be by coincidence, that the examples stated match your situation in the market, or your product, offering or portfolio of services. Of course, there is a general guideline, but a KAM-process must contain detail and be adjusted to your current or planned situation. There is no "one size fits all"-approach.

Design the optimal process for your company, following your new structure to reduce frictions and foreseeable delays when dealing with your key accounts.

# 6. ESTABLISH A KAM-MIND-SET

Key Account Management in the pharmaceutical industry is not simply another sales technique. It is a step towards a renovated business-model. Professional KAM only will work if people adopt a specific mind-set, vastly different from the "pill-pushing era" of the past.

Cross-functional collaboration, sharing expertise and know-how, a value driven approach, delivering something "beyond the pill", and playing a much more active role in healthcare will need change in the heads of many. Any involved protagonist and Key Account Managers themselves need a specific mindset. Again, the competitive advantage will emerge through differentiation from your competitors. You will have to develop and define your own idea what the necessary mind-set, expected traits, and individual behaviours must look like.

# 7. FIND COMPETENCIES NEEDED

Having the right people on board depends on a solid competency[23]- or skills-map and model. Your Human Resource people will help. The relevant accounts, your KAM-process, the mind-set needed, and the specific situation of your business all play a role to draw a competency-map. There may be legal requirements like a medical degree and various soft skills depending on your internal structures. If you see your current structures best described with *silo-organisation* a set of managerial skills and networking ability is vital. In case the matrix-organisation is agile and working optimally, a core skill should be the ability to convey, spread and entertain enthusiasm.

# 8. DEVELOP YOUR PEOPLE

Along this list of expected competencies, skills, and traits your Human Resource-business partner will carefully identify the profile of internal candidates and mirror them against the expected list. HR distinguishes between trainable competencies or skills vs. hardly changeable traits. They will let their business-partners know who from the existing staff can be developed or who the best external candidate will be. Training and education concepts will have to immediately follow any gap analysis.

# 9. SET OBJECTIVES

Anyone in this world starting a journey needs to have a fixed point where to head for and end up. KAMs (Key Account Managers) need direction as everyone else. There are many options, and all must have the same rationale: they need to be within managerial reach.

---

[23] possession of sufficient knowledge or skill,
https://www.merriam-webster.com/dictionary/competency

Your "positioning-statement" shall reflect and match any objective. KPIs and commercial objectives that have been applied to salesforces in the past must be seen as inappropriate. Remember that company revenue is a resultant of efforts. Revenue happens outside your company. Therefore, *revenue* and related terms are not the objectives that you can set in this context.

# 10. KAM STRATEGIES

Once it is clear where you want to go or what you want to be, the next set of questions starts with the prefix: "How to get there?" Any answer to this pivotal question: "How will I get there?" you call *strategy*. This definition is derived from the etymological decent of the word *strategy*. This word is related to warfare and can be found in "The Art of War[24]", written around 500 BC.

How to approach which account, how to identify their pain-points, what kind of offer to design (remember: it must be more than a pill-box) for whom and what to discuss with which individual member of the various decision making units, only is a first set of questions.

# 11. TAKE ACTIONS

Many concepts and ideas are moribund or dead, before they have even started to breathe, because actions are taken either prematurely, incoherently, or not at all.

This step of the KAM process is about getting started and going. Planning or taking **actions** before strategies are decided and identified as clear, feasible, and actionable, will lead to a waste of time and efforts.

---

[24] https://en.wikipedia.org/wiki/The_Art_of_War

## 12. LEARN AND REFINE

Getting close to the intended outcome and before closing the loop, it often shows necessary to lean back and reflect. It is about looking through the assumptions made, the strategies developed, and the subsequent actions taken. The central aim is to constantly learn and continuously improve (KAIZEN[25]) by avoiding repeating mistakes and to improve the coherence and consistency of a selected and decided strategy and its subsequent actions.

---

[25] https://en.wikipedia.org/wiki/Kaizen

# POLITICAL LOBBYING

As a sidenote one might see political lobbying as a variation of KAM. Targets of Political Lobbying are lawmakers who can leverage their power in the interests of a pharmaceutical company. Lobbyists are specialists working in the inner circle of law-making. It is important to mention them, since KAMs probably could learn a lot from **how** they work. Lobbyists identify the networks to cover, collect knowledge about the individuals forming the network, find out about their function and role.

Then they invest time to design and formulate what assumedly shows value to their targets and political stakeholders. Lobbyists carefully plan each step, and patiently pursue their objective. Many of these steps and details applied in lobbying mirror the puzzle-pieces of professional Key Account Management.

Originally, "pharma lobbying" was understood as conveying medical and pharmaceutical expertise into the sphere of politicians. This was done to assist lawmakers making proper and knowledge-based decisions. Today the amount of effort and money invested gives some indication that lobbying at least is partially in the hands of marketing.

Politicians can heavily influence registration and overarching legal frameworks. Therefore, the investment for political lobbying, for example in Washington, USA, is enormous.

Similar approaches to influence politics are on the rise in other places as well.

| Industry | 2018 Lobbying (Through Q3) | 2019 Lobbying (Through Q3) | Percent Change |
|---|---|---|---|
| Pharmaceuticals/Health Products | $218,018,276 | $228,149,734 | +5% |
| Electronics Manufacturing & Equipment | $112,462,614 | $119,190,792 | +6% |
| Insurance | $119,771,068 | $117,358,812 | -2% |
| Oil & Gas | $96,299,274 | $92,164,920 | -4% |
| Electric Utilities | $93,324,015 | $88,428,527 | -5% |
| Business Associations | $104,828,826 | $86,149,006 | -18% |
| Air Transport | $71,855,020 | $79,143,595 | +10% |
| Hospitals/Nursing Homes | $75,685,656 | $78,503,636 | +4% |
| Securities & Investment | $74,486,058 | $75,468,343 | +1% |
| Misc Manufacturing & Distributing | $72,807,696 | $73,618,199 | +1% |
| Health Professionals | $69,788,107 | $73,250,769 | +5% |
| Telecom Services | $68,086,850 | $72,127,000 | +6% |
| Real Estate | $88,597,569 | $65,667,274 | -26% |

**EXHIBIT 13: INDUSTRY LOBBYING SPENDING** .org.

*"Drug companies poured £57m into UK patient groups who research and lobby for new treatments into specific conditions – in many cases the same drugs being marketed by their donors. An investigation by Bath University researchers into donations by big pharma and other industry bodies found the number of donations between 2014 and 2016 rose by a third and the value more than doubled."[26]*

If KAMs have a chance to meet pharma-political lobbyists, it could be a unique chance to learn. How they identify political networks, what they know about individuals forming such networks, and how they design, prepare and approach these people.

Processes in political lobbying deliberately designed or applied by instinct, are very similar if not the same as those, to be applied in Key Account Management.

---

[26] https://www.independent.co.uk/news/health/big-pharma-drug-companies-uk-patient-charities-lobbying-a8925921.html

# ACCOUNT OR WHAT?

We will stick to the wider aspects of Account Management at this stage. This means that we will include all those entities indicated above into the scope of the detailed elaboration of Key Account Management in Pharma.

It is important that a company finds answers to the question how they want to cope with each of these entities. As a rule, and generally the best way to identify possible accounts, you walk along the **approval chain** and drill one or more steps further into detail. However, by their nature, the entities and organisations along this chain are accounts.

---

*Remember: An account is an entity, institution or network in which the decision-making about registration, listing, reimbursement, purchasing, usage, or recommendation of a product or service involves a number of people.*

---

# REGISTRATION

This step deals with the registration or approval of a drug or product. The procedure itself is complex, highly regulated and widely standardized. The outcome of the procedure is determining if a product in the future can be made available to patients and their healthcare providers. It is about marketing authorisation.

Registration bodies have competence either for one or more countries. In any case, there is a number of people involved, who have to make the mutual decision: a drug's benefit outweighs its risks. A number of subject matter experts have to get a clear picture about various aspects and finally vote "yes" or "no" or even a qualified registration like "breakthrough status", or "conditional approval" or "accelerated approval" etc..

## 1.1. National registration offices

In most countries, a national body decides to approve a drug or a medical product. This is a binary on-off decision, allowing a product going to market or not. In the USA this is the Food and Drug Administration (FDA), in China it is the SFDA or now the National Medical Products Administration.

In Europe the deciding body is the European Medicines Agency (EMA) located in Amsterdam. Each European country has its own entity, which in Germany is called the BfArM - Bundesinstitut für Arzneimittel und Medizinprodukte.

## 1.2. Supranational offices

Europe may serve as an example for a registration procedure covering more than one country. The European Medicines Agency (EMA), has moved to Amsterdam after the UK has left the European Union. "The mission of the European Medicines Agency (EMA) is to foster scientific excellence in the evaluation and supervision of medicines, for the benefit of public and animal health in the European Union (EU).[27] Once a product received marketing authorization by EMA, this marketing authorisation covers all 27 European Union (EU) member countries.

---

[27] https://www.ema.europa.eu/en/about-us/what-we-do

# PRICING AND REIMBURSEMENT

Once marketing authorisation has been positively decided, in many countries reimbursement is another "conditio sine qua non". It may be a prerequisite to gain access to the market and achieve reasonable revenues.

In markets where the military, governments, statutory health insurances, or other payers play a role, achieving a reimbursement status is a binary on-off decision.

Take the pricing / reimbursement example of Turkey: The government compares ex-factory prices in a number of other low-price European countries. These currently (2014) are Portugal, Spain, Italy, Greece and France. The lowest of these prices is the Turkish reference price. The ministry of health declares a percentage of the reference price as the ceiling price. This means that Turkish reimbursed prices are below other European prices. The people who contribute to the decision on the markdown of reference prices, are crucial to know and constitute the link between pricing and Key Account Management.

## 1.3. Provincial decision making

Regionalization is the "word of the day" in many countries. Centralized governments are delegating power to form and shape healthcare with regional entities. In countries like Russia, three political or geographical levels of responsibility exist: federal, regional and municipal. Budgets for healthcare are controlled at the respective level. For seven major "orphan diseases" like hemophilia and multiple sclerosis, funding / reimbursement decisions are made at federal level. Russia consists of 83 regions spreading across 11 time zones. The economic and developmental differences are huge. Therefore funding, reimbursement, and pricing decisions may be made and set at a provincial level. This could be an important reason, to establish a regional structure for key account management. In any case it is a good idea for a pharmaceutical company to identify, map and know any of these decision-making bodies and their individual stakeholders being part of the decision-making unit.

## 1.4. National Decisions on reimbursement or pricing

In case of national decision-making bodies, keywords like Health Economics and Outcome Research (HEOR) or Health Technology Assessment (HTA) surface. Usually, a company needs to follow strict and well-known procedures when trying to convince regulatory bodies of the value added to patients and the improved outcome of care with their new product. Especially when the price envisioned is higher than the current "gold standard" of treatment.

In ever more cases, especially for chemical drugs, the gold standard is represented by a generic. Only if there is enough evidence of a better outcome, a reasonable price for a new chemical entity will be accepted. By its nature ideas of value and pricing concepts about novel drugs or NCEs vary significantly between pharma and payers.

The number of products not launched or withdrawn from the market due to pricing issues or denied reimbursement in specific countries is growing.

After the first biological drugs lost exclusivity, pricing even in this field of therapy became a hot topic. Late 2018, less than two months after losing exclusivity for Humira® (Adalimumab) the NHS in the UK entered into a deal with Abbvie. Hospitals in England will see their £400m annual spend on AbbVie's Humira slashed by around 75% over the next three years, thanks to a commissioning deal. The deal involved five biosimilar manufacturers. These kinds of deals are prominent and typical examples for successful Key Account Management.

# THERAPY RECOMMENDATION

Some call it KOL-management. When marketeers believe that the success of a compound or remedy depends on high-ranking scientists or medical opinion leaders, they go after them. If you are one of those working with KOLs, be reminded that no opinion leader in the world is alone, only acts on his own behalf or as an individual. All opinion leaders are part of a group, an entity, or an organisation. By itself, this establishes the assumption, that KOL-Management as it is called, should be established, structured and executed following standardized Key Account Management rules and procedures.

KOLs are embedded in teams or peer groups, researching, and contributing to therapeutic guidelines, conducting clinical trials, or teaching.

Today KOL-management in pharma is a regular discipline or even the name of a specific department. This especially applies to the research based and biotech industry. Objectives, tasks and the geographical positioning of KOL-departments on the organization-chart vary. Often these departments are linked to medical or medical science liaison. In essence and irrespective of who is accountable for KOLs-management in the company, account management procedures apply.

There is yet another similarity with Key Account Management: not all opinion leaders are KEY opinion leaders. Again, there is a clear need to define what is meant with OL or KOL. Very much the definition of who is an "opinion leader" will depend on the product, the therapeutic area, or your company's requirements. In any case, the decision if someone is an Opinion Leader, depends on those, whose opinion is lead, formed, or influenced.

Declaring a person an Opinion Leader because he publishes a lot or because you believe you need him, does not yet qualify an Opinion Leader.

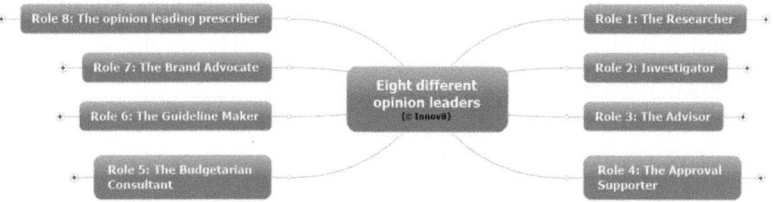

**EXHIBIT 14: EXAMPLE FOR OPINION LEADER CATEGORIES**

*The attribute "Opinion Leader" means that peers and other members of the respective community know, value, adopt, and are influenced by her or his opinion.*

Dealing with, visiting, talking to, or supporting opinion leaders, needs wise differentiation. There are many options how to differentiate, distinguish or categorize opinion leaders. The eight different roles of KOLs can probably play a role in your KOL-strategy?

### Role 1: The Researcher

Researches biological or biochemical backgrounds

WHAT HE OR SHE DOES:

He or she researches if biological or biochemical assumptions are valid in human beings. He or she executes pre-clinical trials and phase I. He or she shares ideas about clinical endpoints. He or she will publish his findings in reputed journals and trigger discussions in international symposia.

He or she chairs a research institute. He or she is a reputed author or co-author for Lancet, NEJM and other high-level publications. He or she is a globally reputed researcher in a specific disease area. He or she carries and follows high-standard ethical values. He or she does not accept industry bias.

## What he provides to us:

He or she ensures that the intended research is in line with the current state of the art. He or she stands for clear deliverables. He or she delivers undisputable outcomes and results. He or she has access to the necessary infrastructure to execute high-level research. He or she provides insights into the mode of action of therapeutic options.

## What he achieves for us:

He or she will raise global interest in the community about the researched subject and related findings. He or she provides robust information on the next steps for trials. The related NCEs or indication areas are discussed and trigger interest. Support for similar trials will be asked for around the globe.

## Role 2: Investigator

Introduces scientific clinical background and alternative / comparative treatment patterns.

## What he does:

In his investigative research he takes novel or different remedies into consideration. His research is driven by comparison and alternative procedures, like PTCA vs. clot dissolving remedies. He or she actively executes and needs funding of clinical trials. He or she regularly publishes his results in respected and reputed journals.

He or she usually works in a university hospital and is specialized in the disease area in question. He or she is a department head or the dean of a faculty. He or she is a member of scientific communities and attends congresses and symposia. He or she is an academic teacher.

## WHAT HE PROVIDES TO US:

He or she delivers support for comparative clinical trials. He or she ensures that various treatment patterns are compared to each other. He or she conveys his findings and the related treatment patterns into the clinicians around him. He or she allows broad insight into the clinical relevance of a treatment.

## WHAT HE ACHIEVES FOR US:

He or she grants interest within his area of responsibility for a new drug and its clinical effectiveness or efficacy. Being a clinician he or she influences others who treat similar patients. He or she triggers the discussion about current state-of-the-art treatment pathways. He or she is a respected and frequent speaker in the individual area of expertise.

## Role 3: The Advisor

Focuses on outcome and advises actionable next steps

## WHAT HE DOES:

He or she travels a lot and advises public institutions and in some cases healthcare industry. He or she publishes findings in international or national journals. He or she conducts meta-trials and researches literature. He or she advises registration and reimbursement bodies.

He or she works in a university hospital as a teacher. He or she is the author of books on diagnosis and treatment. He or she is a fund collector for institution, looking for private-public partnerships. He or she is a frequent speaker in clinical conventions. He or she is a member of public health institutes.

WHAT HE PROVIDES TO US:

He or she knows a lot about current treatments and their reason-why. He or she provides many contacts within the disease area, irrespective which kind of industry it is. His network of practical and pragmatic clinicians is wide and provides valuable input.

WHAT HE ACHIEVES FOR US:

He or she offers his advice on how to approach the medical community. He or she will make the network available to and play a leading consultative role when an NCE or biological drug comes closer to the market. He or she shares with us clinical experience being close to the requirements and needs of the medical community.

## Role 4: The Approval Supporter

Decides on the approval / registration of the product in a specific set of indications.

WHAT HE DOES:

He or she attends frequent meetings with a number of regional (Americas, Europe, CEE, APAC) bodies responsible for drug approval in a region or a country. He or she may still give occasional lectures. He or she works on his own or as associate in a team of a political expert panel. He or she decides about market access of specific medications.

WHAT HE IS:

He or she is an associated member of an approval body like the FDA, BfArM, EMEA, PMDA (JPN) etc. He or she might be an emeritus of a university hospital and his major subject is pharmacology and biometry.

WHAT HE PROVIDES TO US:

He or she allows deep insight into current and future requirements for the approval and got-to-market of drugs. He or she assists in finding and indicating the important wording of key documents. He or she will facilitate contact to other members of the registration body.

WHAT HE ACHIEVES FOR US:

The time to approval is critical and the sequence of approval projects might be in his or her hands. The assistance might help us to improve the marketing authorization application process within the company and help us design internal processes.

## Role 5: The Budget Consultant

Member of a body deciding on national / local budget access / reimbursement.

WHAT HE DOES:

He or she works in an independent institution as a head of department. He or she carries responsibility for healthcare fund budgets or taxpayer's money concerning the reimbursement of drugs (NICE, IQWiG, HAS). He or she can be a member of either a national (France) or regional / provincial (Spain / Canada) or territorial (PCTs, UK) body. He or she influences health policy in terms of cost-benefit and treatment accessibility.

He or she talks about the current political situation and rules and regulations or prerequisites to achieve reimbursement status. He or she can let us know against which standard we need to compare our candidate. He or she decides on the rules the body follows, how prices are negotiated or set or when reimbursement is a binary on/off decision.

WHAT HE IS:

He or she is an expert in health economics and outcomes research representing a specific macro-political direction. He or she holds a specific view on health technology assessment and might have a macro- or microeconomic background and earlier chaired a university institute in economy and / or medicine.

WHAT HE ACHIEVES FOR US:

He or she can be of ultimate assistance sharing knowledge when reimbursement is in question. He or she will direct our efforts into the direction seen as promising and allow appropriate study design. He or she could assist in the necessary analysis and our wording to gain reimbursed status.

## Role 6: The Guideline Maker

Member of a body that formulates standard treatment procedures or protocols.

WHAT HE DOES:

He or she works in a university hospital specialized in the specific disease area. He or she has published numerous articles on the treatment of a specific disease area, He or she is involved in biochemical, environmental, drug and holistic treatment research. He or she is member of a disease related association.

He or she is a clinician or clinical researcher with acknowledged experience and authority in the respective field. He or she is the publisher of disease specific articles and acts as an advisor and author for standard treatment procedures mostly for out-patients.

He or she is our link into the medical society representing the full biochemical, environmental, pre-clinical and clinical knowledge of a disease. He or she allows in depth analysis about unmet medical needs.

He or she will be able to introduce a new treatment into the respective treatment guidelines and grant access to prescriptions. He or she will be able to win others for the usage of our drugs. He or she can be directive to research in terms of unmet needs or necessary treatment improvements.

## Role 7: The Brand Advocate

Triggers and improves awareness of a new option and allows positive brand perception

He or she works in a teaching hospital and is specialized in diagnosis and treatment of a specific disease. He or she frequently delivers medical education in a regional pattern. He or she decides which treatments he suggests in his understanding and at least uses the INN of our product. He or she designs and executes CME-programs.

WHAT HE IS:

He or she is a clinician employed in a regional hospital, with some experience in clinical research. He or she is an author of articles in national journals related to in- or outpatient treatment. He or she is a skilled speaker with a broad knowledge of local treatment habits.

WHAT HE PROVIDES TO US:

He or she helps us creating awareness for our brand in a dedicated geography. He or she represents a trustworthy source of information about the practical implications of prescribing our drug. He or she can assist in an appropriate wording of messages.

WHAT HE ACHIEVES FOR US:

He or she suggest our treatment to his audience and creates brand awareness. He or she ensures that our drug is positioned appropriately and used. He or she supports our messaging and field work

## Role 8: The opinion leading prescriber

Prescribes himself and initiates prescription of others

WHAT HE DOES:

He or she performs cutting edge diagnostics. He or she triggers and starts treatment. He or she runs CME programs in a dedicated geography. He or she advises colleagues on diagnostic and treatment issues. He or she is a reliable source of information and of problem solving assistance.

WHAT HE IS:

He or she works as a physician in a public hospital or owns / runs a private clinic. He or she is in a senior function and at least presides a ward. He or she is well reputed and appears to be a trusted colleague to other physicians.

WHAT HE PROVIDES TO US:

He or she plays a role that provides business opportunities for us due to his double impact: treating his own patients with our drug and suggesting or recommending our drug for treatment to others. He or she will equip us with competitive intelligence and let us share his experiences. He or she will be ready to participate in phase IV trials.

WHAT HE ACHIEVES FOR US:

He or she can be an important driver of immediate revenue. He or she makes his colleagues prescribe through his recommendations. He or she makes us a respected brand and demonstrates its value. He or she exerts a dominating influence on the preference of our brand

## Alternative KOL categories

Different from above, below categories are selected along a somewhat geographical approach.

LOCAL OPINION LEADERS

Often physicians working in their own office, or a group clinic, need and follow the advice of a respected local colleague. These local OLs work in specialized surgeries, chair a hospital ward, or are university teachers, and carry a specific, positive reputation. Local doctors often refer patients to them and ask questions about diagnosis and therapy. Local OLs usually are specialists, being subject matter experts in their specific disease area.

## NATIONAL (K)OLs

Between a local and national separation there can be other splits in your country or for your company. It simply is another proof that "one size does not fit all".

National OLs play a different role. Below examples may serve as indicative and cannot be fully comprehensive. Please follow your professional instinct and experience asking questions to reflect about whom to identify and declare Key Opinion Leader. In above indicated steps around Registration and Reimbursement, nationally reputed physicians are involved in any case. They are asked for their expert opinion in their specific area. No longer their expert opinion is simply called "diabetes", but they would rather be requested to comment on "DPP-IV inhibitors in the treatment patterns of Diabetes Type 2 in obese patients".

You will find national (K)OLs very normally in university hospitals or research units. Usually national OLs still have clinical / bedside experience, working with patients. This might be one differentiator against international KOLs.

## INTERNATIONAL KOLs

Physicians, often working as researchers, respected by and influencing peers in their community and beyond, usually publish in internationally reputed magazines. They often work in pre-clinical fields and share their results at international congresses and similar events. They might play an important role in the making and deciding of therapy guidelines for a specific disease.

Example:

People who have participated in drafting, writing or updating the therapeutic guideline for obstructive lung diseases (GOLD) are few. They represent a core and essential target group for the industry involved in the respiratory field. Their respective network of subject matter experts spans the world.

# TRANSACTIONAL BUSINESS

Medical-representative field forces" sometimes are called "sales" forces, their members are "sales people", and their task is to "sell".

Since these terms have been applied in the mid 1980ies, each of these terms drives the mindset and culture in field forces – in a wrong direction. A major and backfiring result of the usage of these terms became fully evident driven by the Covid19-pandemic in 2020: the habit of face-to-face visits was interrupted. And physicians found out that their business life is even easier without having to see promotional / commercial representatives.

That a medical field force is told to "sell" is fundamentally wrong, because their usual targets are physicians. Prescribing physicians never buy or bought anything from the pharmaceutical industry. Therefore, even the most commonly applied term "customer"[28] indicating is inappropriate or to be precise: incorrect.

A customer is someone who bought a good, a service, or a right. Before a purchase is completed targets are called "suspects. "One may *suspect* that this individual one day could become a customer. The next level is called "prospect". One may believe that this individual will buy in a nearer future and finally become a customer. The underlying marketing concept is called "conversion funnel" or "ladder of adoption". An individual who has finally executed a transaction is a *customer*.

## Account management is different

Account management is dedicated and directed towards an institutional business and constitutes a commercial approach. Some of the steps in

---

[28] https://www.merriam-webster.com/dictionary/customer

the KAM process are prerequisite for business, others have an immediate commercial effect.

So far, we touched a few steps enabling a transactional, yet regulated drug business. Content and flow of every step so far pay tribute to the nature of drug markets, being shaped by prolific lawmakers. The degree of regulation makes the difference between fast moving consumer goods (FMCG) and Rx-, prescription only, drugs. Lawmakers tend "to hug drug markets into dyspnoea". New laws and regulatory interventions are a burden for the pharmaceutical industry.

The majority of drugs today are interchangeable and low-price commodities. These drugs are called "generics" and usually are prescribed using their INN[29], hardly by their "given name, sometimes boastfully called *brand*. Owed to their nature, generics are produced and offered by a lot of companies and their most common, if not only differentiator, is the price. In most countries the providers of these drugs are selected in price-competitive national or regional tenders.

As a simple consequence, each of the steps of the KAM-process is indispensable when aiming to successfully market generic or originator drugs, or an even more comprehensive offering. Such "more comprehensive offerings" in the past have been called "value adding services".

The next buzzword applied in this context is "beyond the pill". The purpose of any of these exercises is to make your pillbox more attractive and help to differentiate your offering in the marketplace.

All those varying targets, from the approval- to a pharmacy-chain, need a dedicated marketing approach.

---

[29] International Non-proprietary Name

The pharmaceutical industry has invented many different bouquets of concepts, separately for each of these stakeholders.

| Registration entities |
|---|
| • FDA, EMA, SFDA / NMPA etc. |

| Reimbursement deciders |
|---|
| • NICE, HAS, IQWiG, GBA, EDL, ministries of health, regional governments, military etc. |

| Recommenders |
|---|
| • Various kinds of KOLs, therapeutic expert panels, guideline writers, etc. |

| Listing bodies |
|---|
| • HMOs, national or regional entities, hospital groups, payers, etc. |

| Procurement & purchasing |
|---|
| • National distributors, Hospitals and -groups, pharmacy chains, etc. |

| .... |
|---|

**EXHIBIT 15: BY THEIR NATURE, THESE ENTITIES ARE ACCOUNTS**

Today we know, that being accounts by their nature is the lowest common denominator for all those entities and bodies. What must be acknowledged is that an account management process, applied procedures, and tools can be the same along and across the "approval chain" and even beyond. KAM is about institutional business.

# ENTITIES LISTING DRUGS

*"The decision-making role of the prescribing physician is marginalizing."*

Not too long ago, this sentence started to be frequently used and quoted. The consequence was that the so-called sales model of the pharmaceutical industry today must be seen as broken and appears no longer valid. Sending medical reps to physicians trying to convince them to prescribe "my product" hardly will trigger more prescriptions in the future. There are more and more lists determining which drug a physician is allowed to prescribe. Drug lists have widely replaced the physician's freedom to decide which molecule or medication he judges as appropriate for a patient and consequently prescribes.

Right after the diagnosis is clear, the ICD-code identified, there is a therapeutic guideline, evidence-based medicine, a best practice, or a drug-list to guide prescription. Guidance sometimes is mandatory some lists only are suggestions. The lowest common denominator of all lists is that they indicate the medical state-of-the-art, the payer's willingness to pay, and often determine the patient's access to medication or reimbursement.

In many countries and markets, using a "listed" drug is the only way to grant affordability to those in need. The deciding body may be a government or the National Health Service, a private insurance company, an HMO (health maintenance organisation), a statutory health insurance, or any other governmental body. This varies by country, sometimes by state or province.

## Municipal drug lists

Depending on the country, federal, metropolitan or municipal bodies fund the provision of healthcare and grant the availability of drugs. This might depend on tenders which in turn depends on the way drugs are distributed and dispensed. In China for example, most drugs are dispensed through local / municipal hospitals. They stick to lists with "brands" / branded generics or INN-named molecules covering the major disease areas. A prescription of a drug outside the list will take extra efforts to be written and filled. In such cases, the proportion of the patient's out-of-pocket contribution will be high or even 100%. The procurement may be centralized, distribution usually is not.

In January 2020, FirstWord's Mathew Dennis, published this[30]:

*Drugmakers cut prices by an average of 53% in the latest bidding round under a scheme in China that sees public hospitals bulk-buy generic medicines. "Products that won bids in this round of centralised procurement saw a huge price drop, which squeezes out unreasonable overpricing that has existed in drug distribution for a long time," the authority overseeing the programme said. The latest round of bidding involved 33 drugs and 122 companies, with as many as six firms chosen to supply 80% of the total national demand for each medicine, up from three in the previous round. "Overall, the price-fall this time is deeper than the first round," noted ICBC International analyst Zhang Jialin, with the largest price cut coming in at 93%."*

Price cuts of this dimension point towards almost embarrassing margins and the inability to deliver value instead of simple pillboxes. Bids of this kind indicate missing creativity or only the readiness to fight price-erosion.

> The most important domain and operational area for professional Key Account Management is tender business.

---

[30] https://www.firstwordpharma.com/node/1694579

## Regional drug lists

Especially in large or geographically diverse countries, regions and provinces enjoy a wider political autonomy. In so-called mature markets there is a growing political trend towards more regional autonomy as well.

One could observe this in Spain, where the province of Cataluña wanted to get on their own in 2014. Another example was the referendum in Scotland, trying to separate Scotland from the UK following UK's Brexit. Political trends resonate and reach into the area of healthcare. Some national governments delegate healthcare budgets to provinces and regions. One major effect is that drugs must be listed regionally, often as outcome of a tender. Only if listed regionally, a product will be available and accessible for doctors and patients.

## National drug lists

In markets with tax-funded healthcare or countries where healthcare is funded through mandatory / statutory health insurance systems, usually governmental bodies make decisions. Which drugs and medical procedures are covered or reimbursed is a question of tenders and bids. The entrance of a drug or product onto a national drug list is decisive and binary: you are either in or out.

The Essential Drug Lists (EDL) usually are decided on a national level. Leveraging such "EDLs" governments support endeavours to provide basic access to healthcare to all. Covering remote areas and granting healthcare to all is set up in programs like "Universal Health Care (UHC)" in India and promoted by the WHO as "Universal Health Coverage[31]". Changes to lists, the rationale of getting on the list, drugs and diseases involved, develop fast and are manifold. Typically, specific tender procedures like an RFT (Request for Tender) to possible

---

[31] http://www.who.int/universal_health_coverage/en/

suppliers precede the inclusion of a product or treatment in an EDL (essential drug list).

It will be difficult to reverse the trend that price is the only differentiator between drugs. Many generic companies have failed to add any value to their products. As a consequence, in most cases today price or cost are the only relevant topics. Sometimes timely availability of supplies is another determining factor to win a tender.

The first key account manager who will be allowed to offer "value beyond the pill", and win a tender with something else but a simple pill box will earn the merits for the first step into a new world.

# ENTITIES PURCHASING DRUGS

Two catalysts have shown fostering pharmaceutical companies to become players in a real market, consisting of *demand and supply*:

1. The low-complexity commodity's business involving manufacturers producing and marketing a multitude of identical products, called *generics*.
2. Pharmaceutical companies had to be granted the right to conclude contractual agreements with other players in the healthcare arena. This has not always been the case in many countries.

Today many patients are treated with a replacement of an originator's drug. "-Similars" or "-Identicals" without a reasonable risk for the patient are substituted at several levels of the distribution-chain. Substitution happens even if it may still be see as illegal.

This applies to generics and many patent-protected drugs, having the same or similar indication or being of the same "species". Substitution of prescribed drugs has a long tradition in some pharma-markets and is more and more everyday reality.

One must admit that it does not make a lot of sense to physically distribute too many different drug-packs containing drugs with the identical molecule. To establish and provide the full supply-chain for x-different Diclofenacs or a multitude of Amoxicillins is unnecessary and far too complex for pharmacists and wholesalers.

---

*If your generic or biosimilar is listed, has reimbursement status and is prescribed, there still is no guarantee, that patients will get exactly your product.*

---

## Wholesalers

Each wholesaling company by definition is an account, sometimes even of key relevance and importance. Missing to spot a wholesaler might make you miss a relevant market-proportion and the related influence.

The regions or chunks of the total market covered by a wholesaler often are unknown and carry surprises. There is no way or automatism forcing a wholesaler to order, buy, sell, and distribute a listed product.

Wholesalers are professionals in logistics, very well aware of where and how value can be created along their specific "value chain". In addition, their profit margin in general is lower than what a pharmaceutical company is used to. They know about the benefit of streamlining their warehouses.

If a pharmaceutical manufacturer wants to be successful, wholesalers need to explicitly be known, must order and distribute your drug or portfolio. Only then they can positively affect your P&L. Sounds simple, is not. Key account management is the best possible tool to make it happen.

## Distributors

The division line between wholesaler and distributors may be blurred. Both words can mean the same, but there are countries like the Philippines, where distributors cover more of the value chain than only buying and providing drugs to a pharmacist. There are distributors executing marketing and sales tasks for pharmaceutical producers. In such a case, their portfolio of drugs will be limited and show conflicting interests with other manufacturers. The distributing company may not want to harm their existing business by taking your newly listed product on stock. The task for a key account manager is to make sure that a distributor explicitly orders and distributes your products. You surely can imagine ideas or concepts which would support the wholesalers business establishing you as their preferred partner.

## Pharmacy chains

Pharmacy chains are established or allowed in many, not in all countries. There are places where the provision of drugs 24/7 to patients in need is not only seen as a business, but a societal duty. Pitifully in the last decades pharmacists have been degraded to merchants in many places. The Pharmaceutical industry to an extent is to be blamed for their declining reputation.

Their role is regaining importance, as is their reputation. They belong to the guild of Health Care Professionals, regularly and actively supporting physician's prescriptions. Pharmacists should therefore be valued partners in the delivery of care.

They give advice to patients and are widely seen as a trusted species. Referring to pharmacy chains, there are countries showing oligopolistic tendencies, having only few pharmacy chains providing drugs. These professionally managed chains usually offer more than drugs to their customers as a matter of institutional competition. Their services are numerous and their need for improving and innovating is considerable.

Most commonly they have a centralized purchasing or procurement unit. Their advantage over pharma is their direct and immediate contact to patients through every single of their pharmacies. The pharmacy-chain headquarter needs to agree on your offering and make sure that, irrespective of a physician's prescription, that your product is dispensed as long as legally possible and medically feasible.

## HMOs

*In the United States, a health maintenance organization (HMO) is a medical insurance group that provides health services for a fixed annual fee. It is an organization that provides or arranges managed care for health insurance, self-funded health care benefit plans, individuals, and other entities, acting as a liaison with health care providers (hospitals, doctors, etc.) on a prepaid basis. The Health Maintenance Organization Act of 1973 required employers with 25 or more employees to offer federally certified HMO options if the employer offers traditional healthcare options. Unlike traditional indemnity insurance, an HMO covers care rendered by those doctors and other professionals who have agreed by contract to treat patients in accordance with the HMO's guidelines and restrictions in exchange for a steady stream of customers.* (Wikipedia, 2020) There might be something analogue in your country.

District health organizations in India for example could show the same challenge for covering and ordering drugs, after they are listed. Each HMO needs to explicitly approve reimbursement and subsequently provide your drug to patients. Only then, reorders and revenue will happen.

## HCP conglomerates

There are numerous legally possible and corporate designs when Health Care Providers cooperate. Let it be group practices, private and other clinics with many physicians and nurses, or long-established networks referring patients between each other. The clinical commissioning groups of the NHS[32] may be one of these examples. These formal or informal networks involve many different disciplines, medical specialties, care and rehabilitation experts, nursing, and

---

[32] https://www.nhscc.org/ccgs/

homecare services. In all regularity partners will agree on a list of drugs or products they use for most of their patients.

After the number of patients can be high, such HCP conglomerates may well earn the status Key Account. They need to explicitly approve your drug, before it can be made available for reimbursed prescription within the conglomerate or HCP-organisation.

## Hospitals

Hospitals usually are owned and run by public or private investors. The Charité[33] in Berlin for example is the biggest single hospital in Europe.

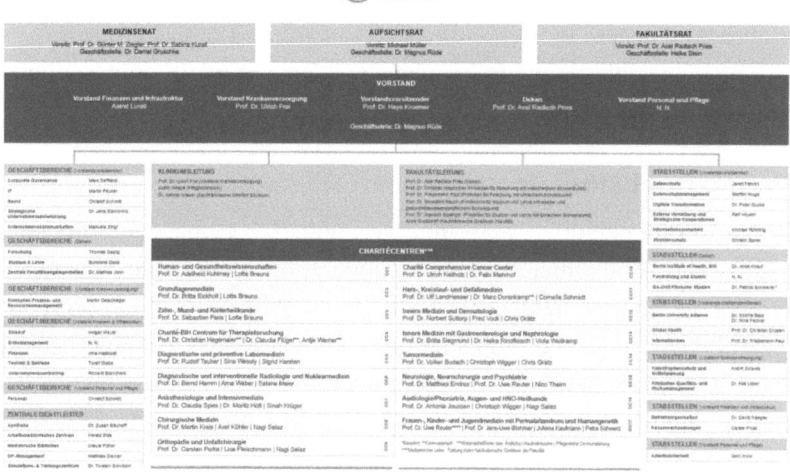

**EXHIBIT 16: CHARITÉ ORGANISATION CHART**

This university hospital is owned by the City of Berlin. In 2020 the revenue was close to 2 bn Euro.

---

[33] https://www.charite.de

The Helios-group, affiliated to Fresenius[34], owns and runs 86 different hospitals in Germany, treating around 5,2 million patients per year with a revenue of around 2bn Euro as well.

It is easy to imagine, that these kinds of accounts can be of paramount importance for a pharmaceutical company's economic success. In all these cases, the procurement of drugs and other products is centralized.

In the case of Helios, it is a remarkable and strict rule, that no industry-representative is allowed to visit physicians or other targets in any of their hospitals, without the explicit and rare permission of Helios HQ.

This means that a perfectly orchestrated Key Account Management is vital to gain access to such entities. To establish a relevant business is no longer possible, trying to convince residents, medical or operational directors on site.

**Pharmacy-chains**

Similar to hospitals, and pharmaceutical companies, mergers, acquisitions, and other forms of cooperation are on the rise when looking at pharmacies. Walgreens Boots Alliance[35] may serve as example for a huge and global network of own and served pharmacies. They own more than 18,750 stores in 11 countries and run one of the largest global pharmaceutical wholesale and distribution networks. More than 400 distribution centers deliver to more than 240,000 pharmacies, physicians, health centers, and hospitals each year in more than 20 countries. Undoubtedly Walgreens Boots Alliance should be one of the few global Key Accounts for a pharmaceutical company, looking for a similar reach across the world.

---

[34] https://www.fresenius.com/
[35] https://www.walgreensbootsalliance.com/

In a traditional setting, few pharma companies have ever considered wholesalers as relevant. They were those entities who purchased and procured the drugs prescribed by a physician to the respective pharmacy. There was little choice in the past.

Today this world has changed: Pharmacists nowadays can substitute prescribed medications if there is a "similar" or "equal" available. This is especially relevant in countries like Germany, India, China and many others, where drug-therapy widely relies on generics. It is the pharmacist's or the pharmacy chain's decision, which of the generics of either kind will be dispensed. A pharmaceutical manufacturer's revenue today often depends on the good-will or contractual agreements between pharmacy-chains and manufacturers.

## USAGE OF A PRODUCT

After all thresholds and steps indicated above are surmounted, the use or consumption of a product or drug will be the final achievement.

**Remember:**
We are still talking about Account Management. A goal of Account Management is permeating healthcare organizations in the pursuit of establishing a lasting and value adding bilateral business relationship.

Account Management is about professional Business to Business (B2B) and sometimes will even allow the co-creation of products or services. However, when it comes to the usage of a medical product or drug, probably the major and most significant decision maker is beyond a company's or a KAM's reach: it is the patient.

Multiple research shows that the patient rejects around 50% of drugs prescribed and(!) dispensed or paid. This huge problem is called non-adherence. Following a comprehensive analysis of the situation around non-adherence elaborated by Cap Gemini in 2012, the pharmaceutical industry misses a lot of revenue decided by patients:

*"Our estimate of $188 billion in pharmaceutical revenue lost annually in the US alone and $564 billion globally due to medication non-adherence is the most accurate estimate to date."* (Thomas Forissier, 2012)

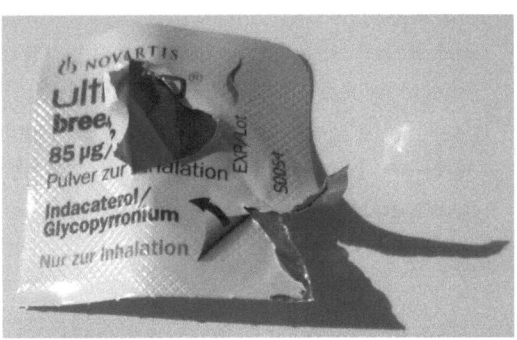

**EXHIBIT 17: CX-USABILITY UNKNOWN**

The topic will pop up later again, as this could be one of the most pressing problems and issues for the pharmaceutical industry and for healthcare as a whole. It can be an area for most valuable cooperation between patients and industries. Testing drugs and their packaging in a usability lab alone could improve therapeutic adherence a lot. (example of non-usability above)

### Hospital wards / departments

Once the hospital or hospital-chain has approved to list your product or drug, the next step to be exploited in the value chain is the ward and the people working there. The bottleneck to achieve revenue is changing the habitual application or usage of whatever was prescribed to in-patients before your product started to be available.

Remember:

*Patients have been treated <u>before</u> your product was available and patients will receive treatment, even if your product is inexistent.*

If the product is on the drug-list in the respective institution, the challenge is to ensure that your product is "demanded," requested and used by bedside physicians and nurses.

Again, this indicates room for services unknown so far. Delivering drugs directly to the ward instead of putting it on the table of the central pharmacy may be worth a thought and subsequently a contractual agreement. Although this would need some rare and digital skills.

**Physicians – the final authority for prescription**

In most countries across the globe responsibility for the treatment pattern still lies with the prescribing physician. Decisions about treatment follow specific patterns, determined by the physician's knowledge, his individual experiences, his habits and the assumed or explicit demands from the patient and limited or fostered by the availability of a drug / product.

A physician's role is marginalized by guidelines and more and more other interferences. Talking about institutional B2B, there are two sides of the coin:

The employed physician only can prescribe what is available, and successfully went through the "approval chain".

Because we are in the field of healthcare, there will be more than one drug or product available for a specific condition.

It is well understood that this is not the case in the field of orphan or areas of rare diseases.[36] This means that a prescriber not only needs an approved drug but should prefer your product or drug over others. Preference building is both a challenge and an immanent part of the approval chain. Every physician needs to explicitly accept, approve and prescribe your drug.

Caveat: The word "selling a drug to a physician" is inappropriately misleading mindset and actions. It is a wrong term frequently used in this context.

### Nurses

"Prescribing nurses" exist in many countries. They have the right to issue repetitive prescriptions to patients without immediate supervision or countersignature by a physician.

In other markets, nurses in hospitals or doctor's offices play similar roles: either they administer a drug, or they assist in prescribing, or at least the repetition of prescriptions. This applies both to in- and out-patient treatments. The influence they have on their doctor cannot be estimated high enough. The same applies to their influence on patients. It is highly advisable that you ensure that nurses explicitly accept and support your drug as well.

---

[36] e.g, "… any disease or condition that affects fewer than 200,000 people in the United States"

## Pharmacists

No matter if a pharmacist is working in a hospital pharmacy or runs his own pharmacy, the drug once ordered and purchased, will only then cause revenue in your books, if the drug is moved across the counter. Your product must leave the shelf and be handed over, be dispensed to a patient.

*Pharmacists can promote or destroy your efforts.*

Every pharmacist along the chain of delivering healthcare needs to explicitly accept your drug for being the one to be dispensed. Only then it will be used, consumed and in the best case re-ordered.

# IDENTIFYING ACCOUNTS

The definition of *"account"* is valid:

*An account is an entity, institution or network in which decision making about registration, listing, reimbursement, purchasing, usage, or recommendation of a product or service involves a number of people.*

Below list is indicative to what we call the "**Approval Chain**". Such a flow is part of the overarching value chain. The approval chain is specific to the highly regulated pharmaceutical and med-tech industry.

There are countries which already have made "Digital Therapeutics" subject to the same rules.

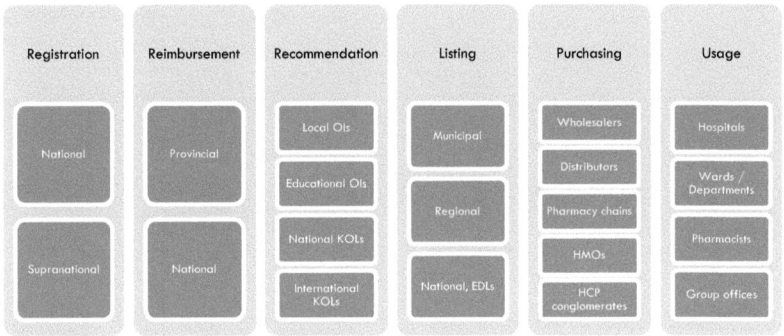

**EXHIBIT 18: APPROVAL CHAIN IN REGULATED DRUG MARKETS**

*The lowest common denominator is that "a number of people" contribute to approval.*

*By definition any of these institutions, entities, governmental bodies, healthcare providing companies, or networks are ACCOUNTS,* irrespective of any other nomenclature.

It may be a point though, to differentiate between commercial and non-commercial accounts. The only difference is the missing transactional nature of non-commercial accounts, like regulatory institutions or KOLs.

Some of these non-commercial accounts might be assigned to units like Market Access, Medical Science Liaison, KOL-Management. They only carry different names. Probably this even is a good idea, since "account" has a connotation of being "commercial". The KAM concept would still apply.

No matter how these entities along the pathway are called, the concept of interacting between an enterprise and any of the above entities in essence should follow the same route as Key Account Management does.

# 12-STEP KAM-PROCESS

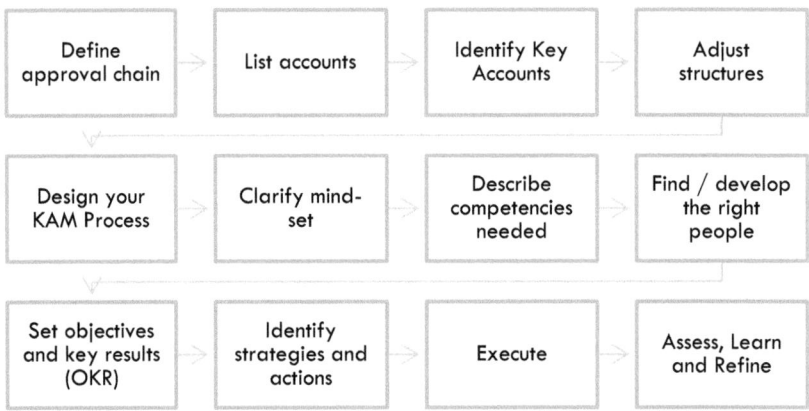

The next pages will follow this flow as a route to success towards a professional, transactional Business-to-Business approach in health care markets, called Key Account Management.

## DEFINE APPROVAL CHAIN

Depending on the offering in question, approval chains vary. Pharmaceutical drugs, prescription or OTC, MedTech products or digital therapeutics follow different routes to gain approval before a supplier is allowed the go-to-market.

## ACCOUNT IDENTIFICATION

The task list allows and ensures easy application of the **Account Identification Process**. Two differentiate work-streams:

1. Preparing the go-to-market
2. Launch

The differentiation respects the current situation in many companies where the word "account" is not applied to those entities, mentioned above as "go-to-market" or "non-commercial" entities. Chronologically these accounts usually need to be addressed <u>before</u> a product or offering is launched.

Remember:
Any entity / account which is not on your list, will vanish being out of your company's focus for a long period of time.

1) Find and map each "go-to-market" step.
2) Find and map each "launch step" after marketing authorization and reimbursement or recommendation is achieved.
3) Collect a comprehensive list of all decision-making entities along both pathways.
4) Identify each entity, which can make binary "on-off" decisions separate for both work streams.

# WHAT MAKES AN ACCOUNT KEY?

In principle all those accounts which make "on or off" decisions about a drug or product, will be key to a company's success. For the majority of regulatory steps, this will be the case. Therefore, these entities by definition are <u>Key</u> Accounts. A similar rule applies to the top three approval steps comprising "registration", "pricing / re-imbursement" and "recommendation".

- Entities in conjunction with "registration", "pricing / re-imbursement" and "recommendation" we call "non-commercial accounts".
  However, their approval is a pre-condition to start any business.

- There is no transactional business involved with them like *"I order, you deliver and I pay."*

- There only is one or few of these institutions per country. This does not make it necessary to differentiate their importance or relevance. They are KEY, because their "on/off-decision" is of vital importance for any further step.

Those who decide about pricing and those influential in the medical community, recommending a drug for a therapeutic guideline, are similarly KEY. Establishing and maintaining regular contact with these entities usually is assigned to individuals or departments like "Drug Registration", "Market Access", or "KOL-Management". Today's structural position of these tasks in the organization chart of a pharmaceutical enterprise may be subject to change for reasons of efficiency and improved cooperation and efficiency.

# HOW TO IDENTIFY KEY ACCOUNTS

There were days when segmenting a market and its players was easy and mono dimensional. Everyone will remember the days of A, B, C, and D. Even in the 21$^{st}$ century there still are companies using this procedure.

By definition Account Management is organisational and reaches far beyond individuals. It is about entities. This indicates that the business figures involved are high.

---

*High volume and high impact are common for each key account.*

---

Please be aware that only few commercial accounts can be key. If Pareto's law serves as guidance, a maximum of 20% of commercial accounts shall be called and treated as KEY account.

## The procedure to identify key accounts

Profiling, Targeting or Segmentation are widely used words in the pharmaceutical world. Some consultants use the words in a different order. Below indicated sample collection of data shows what could be used for "profiling information".

Every year, more than 750,000 people from many countries come to our clinic chain for care.

| | |
|---|---|
| Physicians and scientists working for our patients: | 4,000 |
| Residents fellows and students: | 3,500 |
| Administrative and health staff: | 51,000 |
| Total number of employees: | 8,500 |
| Total number of patients treated: | 1,150,000 |
| Hospital admissions: | 130,000 |
| Total days of hospital patient care: | 625,000 |

**EXHIBIT 19: EXAMPLE FOR HOSPITAL PROFILING DATA**

## Profiling

Profiling is the act or process of collecting information about individuals or enterprises to establish relevant knowledge of business-related characteristics, properties and attributes. Profiling is prerequisite and precedes targeting and segmentation.

Example for hospital profiling:
For obvious reasons it is necessary to know the approximate number of patients in your relevant disease area. The total number of patients treated, or the number of employees or associates is similarly helpful to direct interest and investments.

The question: "Which profiling data do we need?" needs to be answered in all detail. It depends on what your offering is.

*"It's not the data and technology that matter. What really matters is how technology, data, and analytics can help salespeople, sales managers, and leaders improve fundamental sales force decisions and processes."* (Andris A. Zoltners, 2014)

Whatever you plan or tend to collect, make sure it delivers value and serves as a sound basis for actionable decisions. Collecting or even buying huge amounts of data does not make sense by itself. You need to have a clear idea which information or knowledge you can draw form data, and if analytics lead to actionable strategies.

Organization charts are helpful and often available in the internet for download. The formal structure of an entity, once displayed in an organization chart, will enable the Account Manager to identify those individuals who contribute and may be relevant players in the decision-making unit.

## Targeting

Targeting is the process designed to define and select the group of enterprises with whom to start and set up a business relationship. Targeting includes the definition of the target market, relevant for the respective offering or portfolio of offerings. The accounts to target are selected from the list of all accounts.

Example:
If your offering is in the area of dermatology, your targeting process defines which accounts are reasonable to plan, start or continue a business relationship.

## Segmentation

Segmentation is the process to divide the identified group of target-accounts into clusters / segments of similar profiles, similar relevance, similar requirements or needs, or similar behaviours etc. The sole purpose of segmentation is to allow the most appropriate creation of optimally designed segment-strategies.

Segment-strategies are made to allow and ensure different approaches per segment. They <u>must</u> vary per segment.

In Account Management, it is evident that distinguishing key accounts from the rest of accounts is a step, which will show a considerable impact, to the accounts and your company. Below example is descriptive. There is not "one size fitting all."

Naming the two or three axis for the segmentation scheme is a challenge and an art. Each axis must be designed to fully reflect your objective and strategy. Defining the axis precisely following your strategy, means laying the foundation for success. The segmentation scheme displayed will make the difference.

---

*Copy / paste from others using parameters used by everyone else, will prevent success.*

---

## Dimension 1 = y-axis

The vertical y-axis normally shows parameters related to the market. This represents two important topics:

1.  You must describe or <u>define</u> your market first.
2.  The y-axis normally shows external parameters.
    They usually are beyond your direct reach and immediate influence.
    Example: A provider's influence on the size, sales, or units of a market is limited, if not fully absent.

Once the market is defined and clear, displaying the accounts on this y-axis will be a pure technical exercise.

This sounds to be a rather simple exercise, which it indeed can be. Yet the definition of the market will determine or at least influence almost any following step. The influence of the market definition reaches from strategic goals, to business planning, to forecasting, to marketing, to compensation.

Not to forget, the definition allows the comparison between many local operating units of multinational companies. Be aware and clear that the definition of the market selected, excludes the "rest of the world" and will narrow your scope in the foreseeable future. Your business intelligence people will investigate exactly this market, trying to avoid distraction by other market sectors or segments.

Case 1 – illustrative only

General set-up: A company is planning to market the first orphan drug for a rare disease. The prevalence for the targeted disease in the population is about 1.2 out of a million. For a country with 80 million this means there are about 100 patients. The number of patients registered and already diagnosed with the targeted rare disease is 63. The y-axis shows the number of possible patients (prevalence) per geography. The internal discussion will reveal if *prevalence* is the preferred parameter, or if the number of *diagnosed patients* can be a valid alternative. The final decision will depend on the company's strategic ability and will to invest in the "market development". This means a company might be willing to increase the number of diagnosed patients, e.g. by an awareness-campaign. The alternative is to look at the "lower hanging fruits" of already diagnosed patients. If this will be the decided strategy, the y-axis could indicate the "number of diagnosed patients." The definition of the market will have high impact on any following step.

Case 2:

General set-up: A company is about to launch a generic, chemical drug in a "mass market". The target market ATC is R03. The company's objective is to gain a reasonable proportion of the molecule's generic revenue.

The market will be defined on the y-axis and the decision needs to answer these questions:

- Will we utilize the whole R03-market, or shall the market be defined by the patent-losing molecule only?
- Will all presentation forms be included or only tablets?
- Will we measure the market in value, or in DDD[37] or in packs, (= prescriptions), or use a different parameter?
- ....

---

*Be clear about the importance of your market definition.*
*Consequences are reaching far into the future.*

---

[37] Defined Daily Dosage

Only few words have more meanings than the word "potential". Potential is omnipresent, meaning something different to everyone. This is why we strongly suggest a clear definition in your organisation. If there is no definition of potential, you may want to adopt the below suggestion:

$$\frac{Market\ size}{weighted\text{:}\ (100 - x)} \ast \frac{Market\ growth}{weighted\text{:}\ 100 - ((100 - (100 - x))}$$

Potential in general is an index, mathematically calculated from a weighted combination of market *size* and market *growth*. The total of both weightings is 100. Each weighting of the two parameters depends on your strategy and offering. For example entering a market with a generic chemical entity after loss of exclusivity, you would weigh the market size at 100 and growth at 0.

Example:
Some years ago, the market for "drug eluting stents" was growing fast in hospitals with cardiology units. Using only the current market size in units or value, would have shown a misleading picture. One would have fully missed the "future champions", using only the market size as determining factor. Combining growth with size makes a lot more sense. This similarly applies to many more markets especially those with novel treatment options.

Even for hospitals or pulmological centers treating rare diseases like IPF (Idiopathic pulmonary fibrosis) you need "market growth" as an indicator. In conjunction with rare diseases, it could be feasible to define the "market" by the number of possible patients as derived from the statistical value of disease prevalence or the number of patients already diagnosed.

Looking at it from a first-in-market company or preparing the launch of a novel, competing drug[38], the perspective of marketeers on the y-axis will make a difference.

If market growth does not carry or deliver a strategic value for your offering, you will only use "market size" by setting the weighting for market growth to 0, when calculating potential.

In such a case, it is a good idea to delete the word "potential" and replace with "market size".

**Dimension 2 = x-axis**

The x-axis of the account segmentation matrix in all regularity shows a parameter, which is within your reach, often associated with result or outcome.

It could indicate revenue or market share achieved. The number of metrics or measures are as many as company strategies. Your choice must match and mirror your strategic approach to the market. If your strategy sounds like "gain a proportion of ..." you could have **market share** displayed on the x-axis. If your board is focused on revenue, you better consider plotting "sales" on the x-axis.

Remember:
We are trying to find a reproducible way to differentiate those accounts, which play a KEY role for your company.

What about "affinity to our company" or "portfolio adopted", or "degree of penetration", or "degree of partnership", or "%

[38] http://www.boehringer-ingelheim.com/news/news_releases/press_releases/2014/16_october_2014.html

of patients treated with our product," or "degree of client satisfaction?"

Try to create scenarios and carefully see what happens and to which degree the x-axis definition will change your perspective and the names of accounts to earn the attribute KEY.

To distinguish and separate accounts from KEY accounts, parameters must fully mirror strategy. The metric displayed along the x-axis must display what you want to achieve. The x-axis must display a parameter within your reach and your influence.

**Dimension 3 = bubble size**

**Remember:** The identification of KEY accounts varies for each company, its strategy, <u>and</u> by product portfolio or offering.

Adding a third dimension increases complexity of account segmentation. The effort pays-off, when it adds value to your business. It will add value, if your aim introducing or executing key account management lies "beyond the pill".

Imagine your approach is striving for a deeper purpose of the Account Management concept: **a lasting and robust business partnership dedicated to improving the delivery of healthcare.**

This really will make another difference. Remember: There is not one size, to fit all. All axis need to be calculated and therefore carry a "numeric value". Below examples what the bubble-size can stand for, are illustrative:

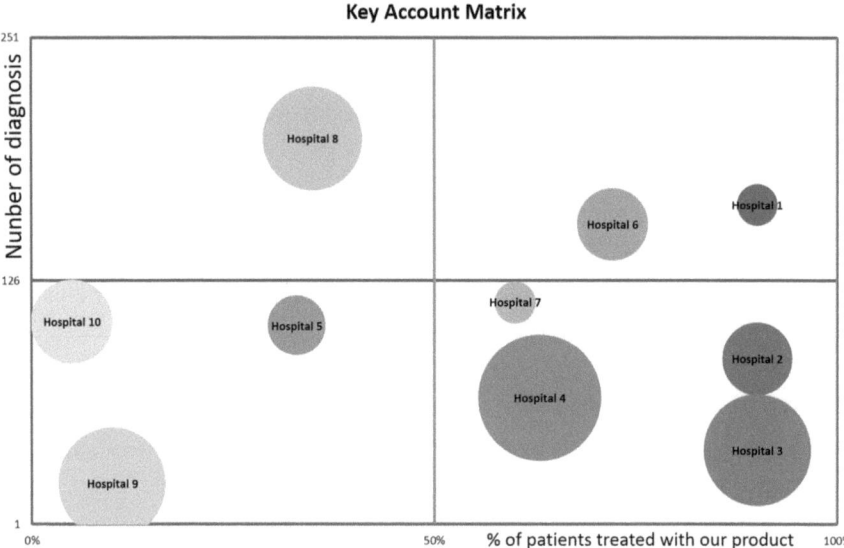

EXHIBIT 20: DESCRIPTIVE MATRIX WITH THREE AXES

Bubble size can describe a "best-guess" of the account's **relevance** for your company.

Bubble size can be a "best-guess" of the account's **importance** for your company.

Bubble size can be a identified facts of the account's **influence on other health care providers**.

To establish individual values carrying significance for you may become a "point-scored" for your competitive advantage, if you use internal expertise. What you "only" need is a "bestimate" (best possible estimation) of a value closest to your strategic approach. The Delphi-Method[39] might help to deliver appropriate results. If you want to start

---

[39] http://en.wikipedia.org/wiki/Delphi_method

or grow your business, the top left segment will show your KEY accounts.

If you need to consolidate your business in a later stage of a product's lifecycle, the top right segment may display your KEY accounts.

Every detail must be clarified, decided and fully support your company's objective and strategy.

## Segment cut-offs

Cut-off lines define the border between high and low, or right and left etc.. It sounds clear but it needs an intentional and conscious managerial decision.

The decision about what you call "high", and what you see as "low". It is an important segmentation step to find a rationale for these cut-off lines. The cut-off lines in the examples we drew at the mathematical mean. This is easy, but not at all mandatory. Yet again, where to set a cut-off, fully depends on each individual company. It is about your offering, the accounts you need to approach, the number or percentage of accounts you want to determine as key, and the ability to assign Key Account Managers to specific key accounts.

The capacity in FTEs (full time equivalents) available or affordable will play a major role in this decision. If you really want to be focused, only having a handful of KEY account in your area of responsibility, you will move the horizontal cut-off line up and the vertical line either right or left, considering your strategic objective.

**Why segment?**

As indicated earlier, the purpose of any segmentation exercise is to allow the creation of appropriate and successful segment strategies. By definition, segment strategies must vary by segment, meeting different needs and requirements. If the strategy for different segments the same, time and effort invested in segmenting is wasted. In the context of identifying KEY accounts, the message is clear: The purpose of the exercise is to assign KEY accounts to KEY Account Managers. Often it is **one** Key Account assigned to **one** Key Account Manager.

Declaration of KEY – example 1

- Assumption 1: The offering has recently been launched and still is in the introduction / growth-phase of its life cycle.

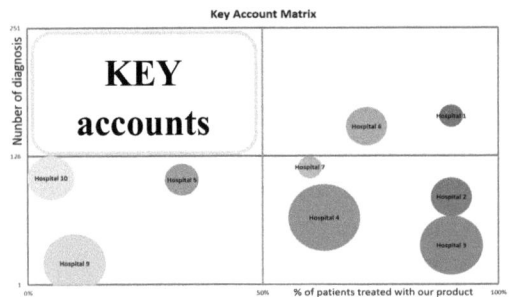

**EXHIBIT 21: SEGMENTATION SCHEME**

- Assumption 2: Company objective is to develop / grow the business into more hospitals treating the respective illness.

These two descriptive assumptions could clearly mark the top left segment as KEY to achieve the strategic objectives.

It is the segment showing the larger market with a small own market share. Reflecting the simplified objective, the segment top-left is KEY.

- Assumption 1: The offering was launched earlier and is approaching maturity in its lifecycle.

- Assumption 2: Objective is to maintain and consolidate the business with hospitals repetitively purchasing.

These two parameters make the top right segment KEY to achieve the objective: *maintain and consolidate.*

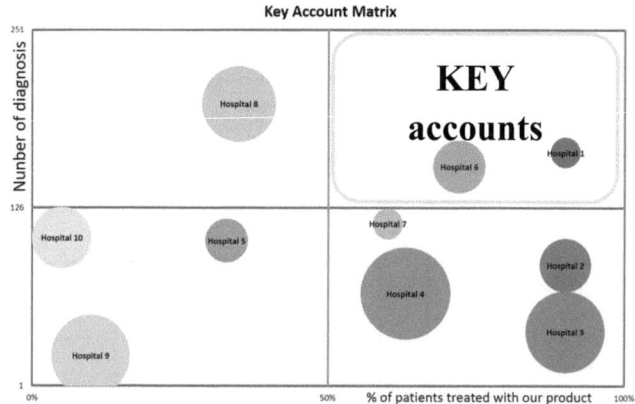

**EXHIBIT 22: SEGMENTATION SCHEME 2**

It is the segment with a large market / high number of diagnosis and a high number of patients treated with our product. Reflecting the strategic objective, the top right segment displays KEY accounts.

## Summary: Steps identifying KEY accounts

This indicates the flow to identify the most important KEY accounts.

After KAM is about lasting and robust business-to-business relationships with few and valuable KEY accounts, many companies deploy or assign one Key Account Manager to one Key Account.

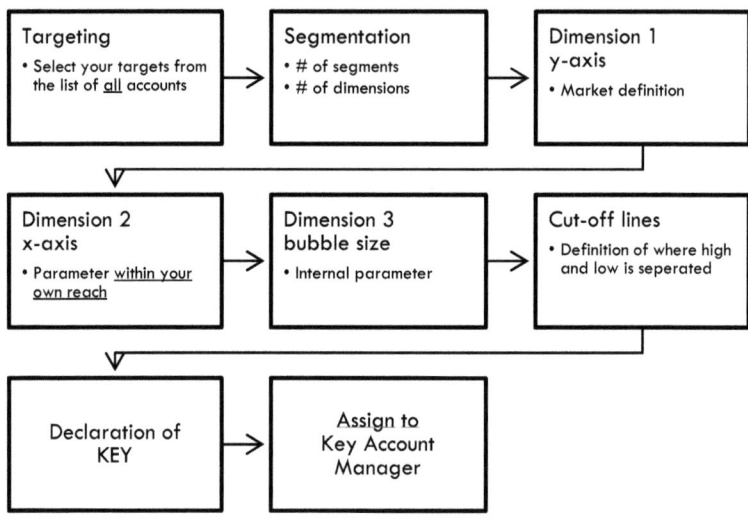

**EXHIBIT 23: DISTINGUISHING *KEY ACCOUNTS* FROM THE REST**

# STRUCTURES IN KAM

---

*Remember: There is no one size, fitting all*

---

Below quote is from Niccolò Macchiavelli, written in the 15th century:

*"There is nothing more difficult to carry out, nor more doubtful of success, nor more dangerous to handle, than to initiate a new order of things. For the reformer has enemies in all those who profit by the old order, and only lukewarm defenders in all those who profit by the new."*[40]

Providing the best possible structures is key to success. A managerial "triple jump" is about three steps being constitutive and dependent on each other:

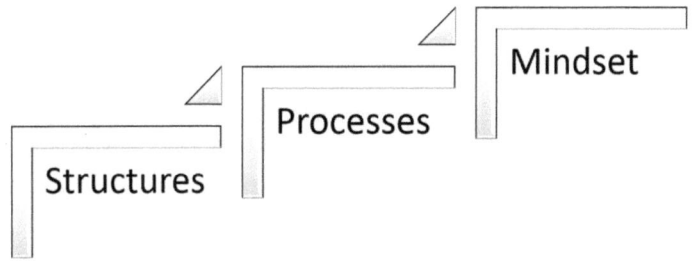

**EXHIBIT 24: A MANAGERIAL TRIPLE JUMP**

---

[40] Attributed to Niccolò Machiavelli

# STRUCTURES

Professional Key Account Management needs cross-departmental collaboration. There hardly is a single person who can meet and satisfy all those needs and requirements, requested by the relevant stakeholders or members of a decision-making unit.

The current organisational structures of pharmaceutical companies still happen to be designed "old-school". There mostly are departments separated by mental walls having been established in the days of defined and separated distribution channels called *Rx, OTC, Hospital, GPs or specialists* etc.

Structures, represented in the organisation-chart, allow and support or prevent and hinder cross-departmental cooperation, necessary for Key Account Management. To involve many internal functions, surmounting existing barriers, cracking the walls between traditional departments, and slashing existing silos is a pivotal step on the route to success.

The suggestion for an organization chart usually is made by external consultants. Pitifully they usually offer what they call "best-practices." This mostly means copy-paste, preventing progress and differentiation.

Some companies set up internal projects to identify the best possible structures. This can be powerful if people involved and affected are asked to actively participate and contribute. C-level management makes final decisions on the structures suggested, inspired by the internal project-team's work and suggested concepts.

# PROCESSES

Designed processes allow effectiveness and efficiency[41]. Traditional processes are established by experience and handed over to the next "generation". It appears evident that in pharmaceutical companies, processes are omnipresent and mandatory in research, development, and production. In marketing and sales, the area of the highest investments and cost, business processes hardly exist or are rarely applied.

The most expensive arena is the traditional field-force. There is no other organisational unit, with more people having the identical job. Everyone does his or her best disregarding procedures and disrespecting distinct processes. Internal best-practices would be great to identify and copy-paste. The internal(!)treasure chest to optimize usually is closed.

# MIND-SET

Achieving the appropriate internal mindset to establish, allow or improve Account Management, requires several steps to make it happen.

John P. Kotter found out that "70% of all major change efforts in organizations fail". (Kotter, The heart of change, 2002).

Assuming that the vast majority of requirements are available it becomes clear that the mind-set is the most crucial point to fill news structures and subsequent processes with life.

"Change Management" is the term usually attributed to attempts or projects attempting to change mind-sets within an organisation.

---

[41] Effectiveness = doing the right thing. Efficiency = doing things right. (P. Drucker)

Everyone trying this must be clear that it is impossible to "powerpoint associates into change". All of us human beings tend to change only, driven or caused by individual insight.

We all touched a hot-stove when we were young, despite multiple requests, orders, even severe penalties did not prevent us from burning fingers".

One must admit that in adult life, this is the same. The only concept driving change in mindset and habits is to design a conceptual approach, allowing to touch a hot stove and burn your fingers in a secure environment.

Exercises simulating consequences of decisions and mindset have shown to be powerful tools.

# STRUCTURAL EXAMPLES

## Traditional pharma

This is a traditional example. A clear dividing line between marketing and sales and between different sales lines keeps distance between units and allows managers to be held accountable for his or her individual results.

Most functions are usually perceived as delivering their internal services to the field-force.

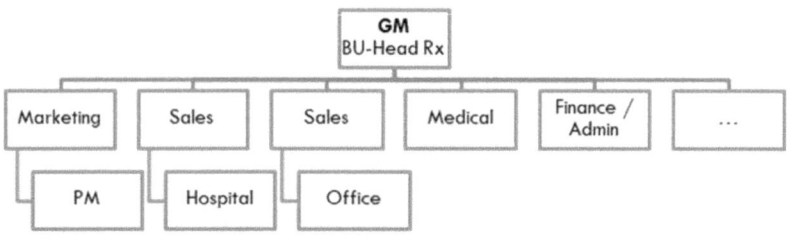

**EXHIBIT 25: TRADITIONAL ORGANIZATION CHART**

Marketing delivers sales folders and -support. Medical delivers or approves what sales wants to communicate.

Finance provides the promotional budget for each medical representative and supports costly congresses and monetary benefits.

This kind of old fashioned "business arrogance" often had its origin in the number of positions and people. Missing collaboration and many silo situations are the major consequences of a structural domination by the field-force.

## Field force collaboration

Rare but it happens: the field force is part of marketing, following the rationale of Philip Kotler's 4 Ps. The field-force's major task is a promotional one.

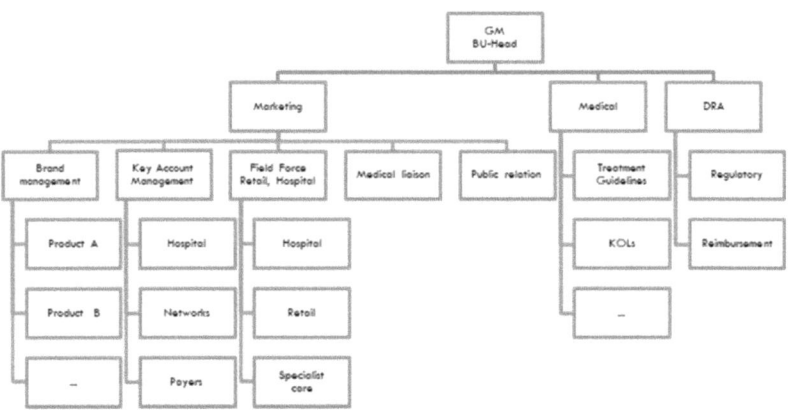

**EXHIBIT 26: COLLABORATIVE STRUCTURE**

In a normal Rx-business only few, if any people, are involved in transactional selling. This allows the assumption that field force's activities are designed to promote prescription a product.

It may be a good idea to have hospital, retail and specialist care reporting to the same management. Their territorial alignment will allow better coverage, identification and solution of local problems. Similarly important is to know connections and relations between all these different stakeholders and healthcare providers in a specific geographical setting.

## Lifecycle focus

The most remarkable innovation in this example is that marketing no longer is structured along the brands but follows the expertise and requirements to effectively manage the lifecycle of products. Oncology as a niche and highly specialized business still is separate.

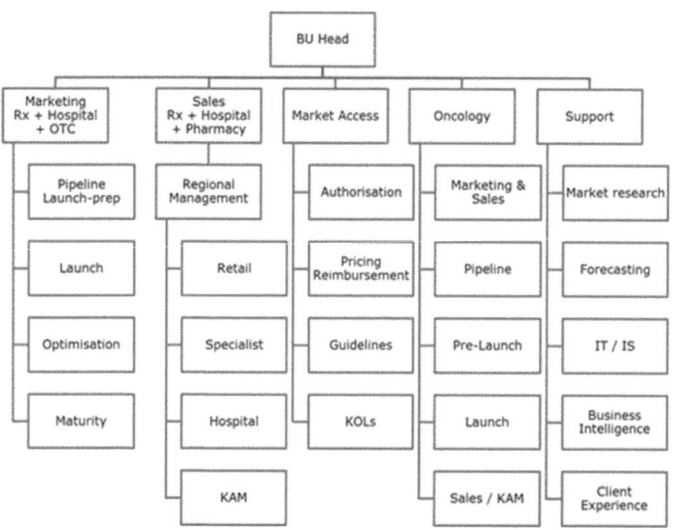

**EXHIBIT 27: PRODUCT LIFECYCLE STRUCTURE**

People in the field are all in one hand, reporting along the same "chain of command".

Market access is covering all species of "non-commercial" accounts.

Guideline making and other KOLs are separate, following the concept of regionalization. Treatment or medication guidelines usually are more or less global.

## Client centric structure

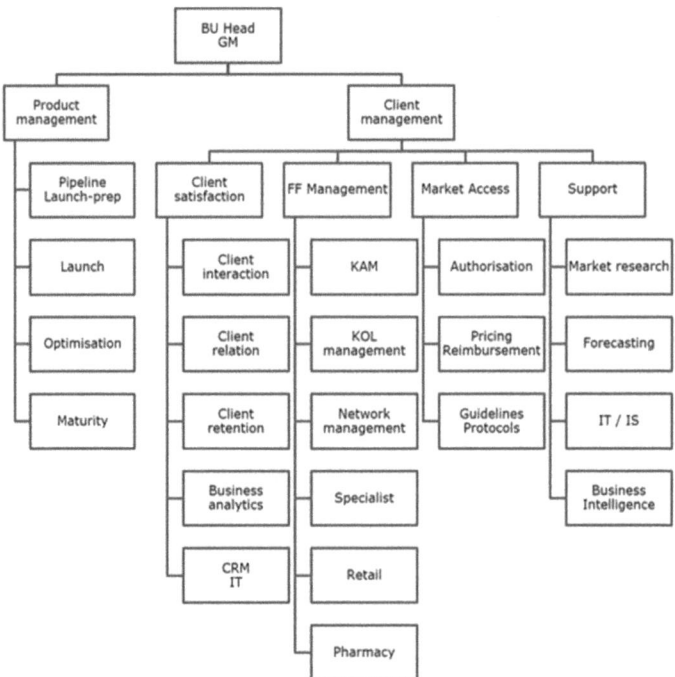

**EXHIBIT 28: COMPANY ORGCHART ALLOWING CLIENT CENTRICITY**

The word "client" is deliberately used. In contrast to *"customer"*, *client* indicates a decisive difference in the world of regulated Rx-drug markets:

A customer *purchases* goods or services; a consumer *uses* goods or services. Whereas a client in many languages is someone having a specific and trusted relationship to a provider.

The word *client* regularly is used indicating the special and often legally protected relation between an advocate and its client. The term "customer" is inappropriate and not applicable in this context.

Above organization chart carries another special and bold detail: the pharmacy / OTC business is an immanent part of this structural design.

TV- and other promotional channels more and more drive the OTC-business. Field force activities in the OTC market no longer are related to "selling" since wholesalers and distributors offer the same or even better purchasing conditions for pharmacists.

Yet, reflecting the patient journey needs the pharmacist.

If KAM is reaching beyond the pill, the pharmacist is a very precious ally for an Rx-pharmaceutical company. The pharmacist is the most frequently seen and the most valuable and direct touchpoint between pharma and the patient. The pharmacist's role supporting therapy adherence in patients is crucial.

# FUTURE PROOF STRUCTURES

*"What is called for is, in fact, the antithesis of undirected restlessness. It is the painstaking infusion of tension to bring about the kind of dynamic imbalance that has always been the hallmark of the successful, growing organization."*

(Tom Peters, 1979)

> *Key Account Management in essence is a team approach.*

If it is within your arm's length, it really is advisable to carefully select a structure, which will enable and support Key Account Management.

KAM will only work being established as cross-functional entity, involving people carrying synergistic competencies.

**Cross-functional collaboration - example**

The automotive industry not only is close to each of us, but also shows great examples in the context of account management, already having changed and continuously changing their business-model.

Other than in the past, automotive manufacturers are offering a lot more than a car today. This does not only apply for their B2B-business, but individual customers are offered mobility solutions instead of a single product.

We do not only buy a car, but a package of goods and services granting mobility. It reaches from insurance, to covering services, to granting mobility, to many kinds of financial services, and insurances. In addition, we are offered a fully customized vehicle.

# AUTOMOTIVE INDUSTRY: BLUEPRINT FOR PHARMA?

Imagine what happens when a global pharma company is inviting tenders for their new car-policy in a European country.

Case description:
The number of employees being equipped with a company car is more than 1,500. Tenders are invited to cover the car-fleet for a period of five years. After 120,000 kms or 36 months, cars shall be replaced.

Depending on legal and fiscal regulations, the touch points[42] for the KAM will look like this:

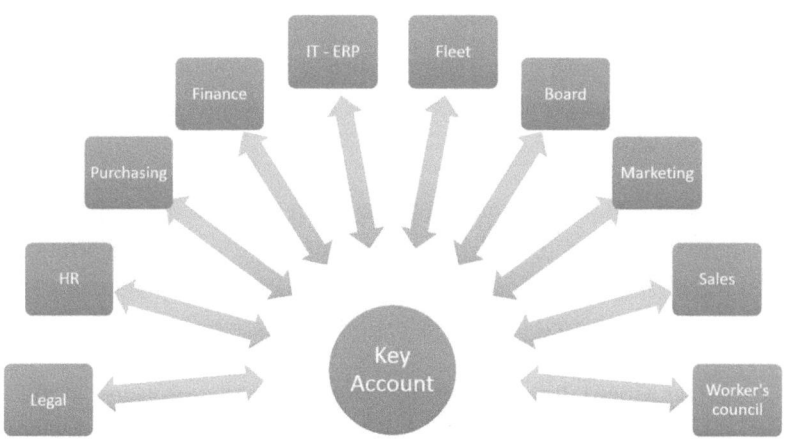

**EXHIBIT 29: LIST OF KAM TOUCH-POINTS**

---

[42] The order of touch points is random

Members of the Decision Making Unit as detected from the automotive KAM's perspective in random order:

1. The account's legal department is needed to design and agree any kind of contractual agreement.

2. Human Resources will play a role in making decisions about how it is possible to mirror hierarchy and factual requirements of the company's car policy.

3. Purchasing wants to know about "total cost of ownership" and the services included.

4. Finance will decide on the company's preferences between buying, leasing or financing. Car manufacturers today carry a full bank license to assist with any financial service needed.

5. IT – ERP will have plenty of demands around data interfaces to allow analytics, comparisons and interfaces to taxation or refunding.

6. Fleet management will ask many questions about their degree of involvement and which slices of the car administration, accident-, repair-, service-, tire- and mobility-management etc. will be covered by the car manufacturer.

7. The Board has a genuine interest in all questions around sustainable use of natural resources and the degree of compliance with environmental protection and social responsibility of the future car fleet.

8. Marketing will want to know all details of brand perception and positioning of the car fleet in the mind of employees and clients.

9. Salespeople will have a close eye on the comparability of their car-fleet with competitor's, the usability in the field and the reputation displayed by the car brand.

10. Worker's councils play a major role in deciding on fairness and if the planned car-fleet and the policy around it is just and reasonable.

The example indicates ten different stakeholders involved in decision-making about the new car brand for the company car. Every unit will have different needs to be clarified and specific requirements to be met. A singular key account manager definitely cannot meet all needs and know all about everything.

One of the KAM's pivotal tasks therefore is to identify the relevant people, collect details about their role in the business, their contribution to decisions, the attitude towards the project, and the anticipated needs and requirements they might have.

The different skills, expertise and knowledge needed to meet all needs in the Key Account is subject to the KAM's assessment and evaluation.

The people needed to win the business and be part of his team, he will detect inside his own company. Participation in such a project must be requested, cannot be mandated, or enforced. The expectations are high. The KAM needs to identify and form a temporary project-team, prepare and execute professional briefing sessions. Once formed, the KAM needs to manage this team on its way to success. This is why these people are meant to be the "gold reserve" of a company but their position has been named Key Account **Manager**.

# DEFINITION OF "PROCESS"

*"A business process begins with a mission objective (an external event) and ends with achievement of the business objective of providing a result that provides customer value. Additionally, a process may be divided into subprocesses (process decomposition), the particular inner functions of the process. Business processes may also have a process owner, a responsible party for ensuring the process runs smoothly from start to finish.*[43]

Most of what we do follows a specific pattern of actions. A distinct pattern of actions only turns to be a *process*, once it is available "on paper" or documented. Documentation of business processes is a mandatory requirement.

1. Relevant employees must be aware that there is a documented process.

2. Documentation of any process must be accessible by those, who have a reasonable interest or are involved in the process.

There are several tools and methods available for business process mapping **and notation** (BPMN). One is Microsoft Flow [44], which can be used for automation of process steps simultaneously to their notation.

---

[43] https://en.wikipedia.org/wiki/Business_process
[44] https://emea.flow.microsoft.com/en-us/

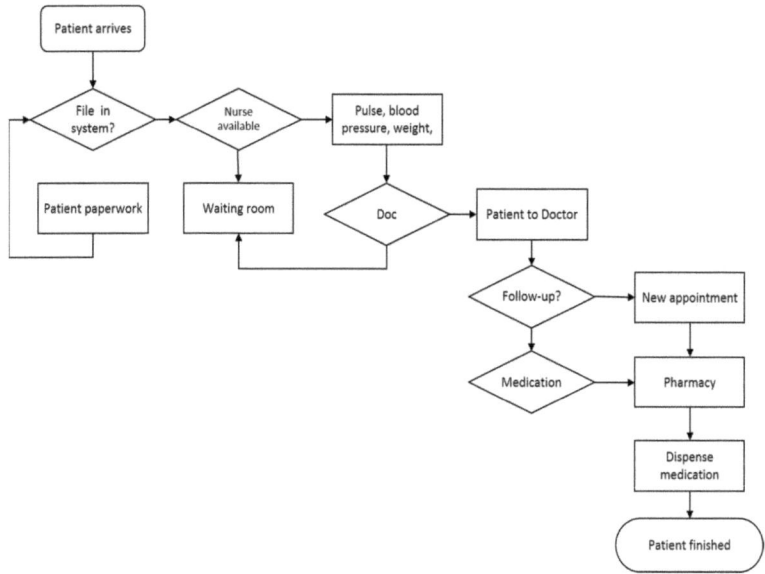

**EXHIBIT 30: SAMPLE PROCESS FOR MEDICAL SERVICES**

*Only when documented, processes can be applied, effectiveness and efficiency improved, productivity boosted, and organization's performance enhanced. Only when documented, processes are available for "continuous improvement".*

The example constitutes such a documented process in the defined sense of the word. The design of flow charts may vary by the tool used or by the intended degree of detail. Any software provides ways and means to draw flowcharts and leverage symbols with specific meanings indicating specific tasks, steps, documents, sub-processes, interfaces, etc. In Key Account Management, processes to be designed and documented is a major task.

# KEY ACCOUNT PROCESSES

*"In professional KAM organizations, the Key Account Managers will analyse the account, its resources, the structure, the processes applied, and their strategic logic. Beyond the key account, they need to fully understand the account's market environment. Hence, KA managers somehow work similarly to "special agents" who collect information about targets and distribute this information inside their own organization in order to improve their own organization's performance."* (Björn Ivens, Catherine Pardo, 2014)

Below indicated flow shows one of many possible ways to design an overarching Key Account process. Documenting such a process will boost many details and ensure a common understanding of all involved. The common understanding of steps and details is of paramount importance. Today it appears to be rare, even within the same company.

## A SINGLE KEY ACCOUNT

*There is no one size fitting all!*

The Individual Account Management steps might or even should vary between you and other companies. The indicated flow might serve as a template or framework to be filled with your individual content.

The sequence of steps may vary and the wording should be adapted to your vocabulary. Remember: the vocabulary used, must be understood in an identical way meaning the same to any of your colleagues.

Because the account is KEY, the process is designed for repetitive application being improved over time. Anything done around such a KEY account should become part of a continuum, continuous improvement.

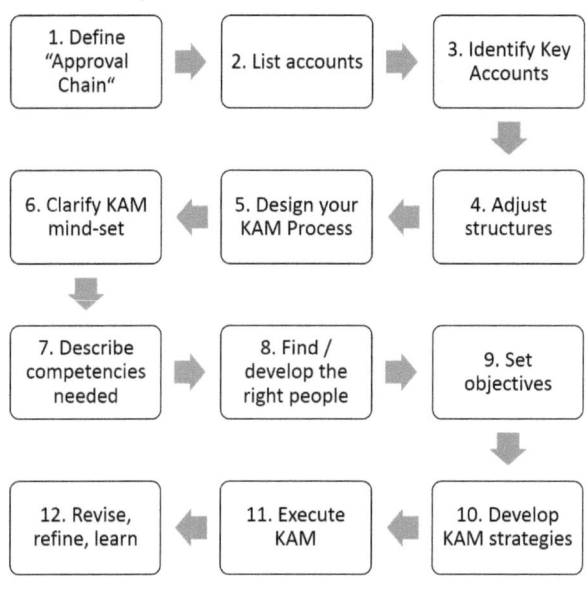

**EXHIBIT 31: KEY ACCOUNT PROCESS**

*KAM is about establishing and maintaining a robust and lasting business relationship.*

"One night stands" to create quick wins, or harvest "low hanging fruits", delivering short-term profits for a pharmaceutical company would thwart the KAM concept. The introduction of professional KAM will surely contribute to more trust for a widely distrusted industry.

*"On trust-building initiatives, pharma companies shouldn't be waiting to follow the lead of competitors — they should be elbowing each other to be the first one out the door."* (Ernest&Young, 2014)

Please remember our definition of *account*: it is an institution, enterprise or entity.

As a company, you usually have more than one offerings. We assume that these offerings will be interesting for different DMUs within the same account. You therefore will have one process dedicated to the account as such, and separate ones dedicated to each DMU.

The Individual KAM-Process is straightforward:

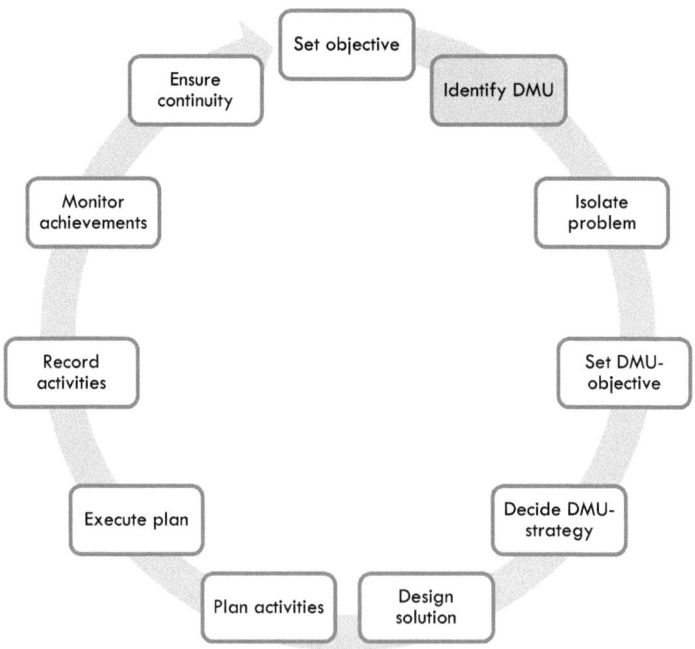

**EXHIBIT 32: PLANNING AN INDIVIDUAL ACCOUNT**

Once you have an idea what to achieve with the individual Key Account, you need to find all those people of relevance. Together with the DMU members and privileged with the KAM's "helicopter perspective", the isolation of a specific problem to be solved with your company's expertise is the next step.

This is directly followed by finding the objective for this **Decision Making Unit**.[45]

How to achieve and meet the objective will lead to the design of an appropriate solution or offering.

The solution available will determine how activities will be planned, followed by their execution.

Activities will be recorded, and achievements closely monitored.

Ensuring continuity in the cooperation with the DMU and the account closes the cycle of establishing a robust and lasting business relationship. The essence of KAM.

---

[45] Buying Center is a synonym for DMU

## Objective setting for an individual account

For good reasons you identified a specific account as being KEY for you and your business. It may be a painful exercise to find and set an objective for your key account. It is far too simple and hardly constructive to take your internal forecasting data and calculate an expected revenue for a specific account.

> *Simple commercial objectives in the sense of revenue, sales, or market share are inappropriate in Key Account Management*

**Commercial success follows the value delivered. It is not the other way round.**

If below definition of management is true, than commercial figures like revenue, sales or market share in an account / other organization anyway are beyond your reach. A manager simply cannot manage what happens outside his walls.

*Management in business and organizations is an art that coordinates the efforts of people to accomplish goals and objectives using available resources efficiently and effectively. Management comprises planning, organizing, staffing, leading or directing, and controlling an organization to accomplish the goal.* (Wikipedia, 2014)

It is helpful and a general rule, that a managerial objective starts with the word: *"Because this account is key for us, we ....."*

Examples for account-objectives:

> *We want to become the preferred provider of medical and therapeutical expertise in this <u>hospital</u>.*

*Based on our medical experience, we will cooperate with the payer-organization on mobile-health topics to improve efficiency of care.*

*We will share our medical know-how to help them improve patient outcome.*

*We will optimally support the wholesaler's collaboration with pharmacies by establishing educational services.*

Any of these account-objectives is worded from the account's perspective and with their needs and benefit in mind.

### Identify the Decision-Making Unit

Following a consistent approach, the very first step is to identify players and stakeholders who are involved in making decisions.

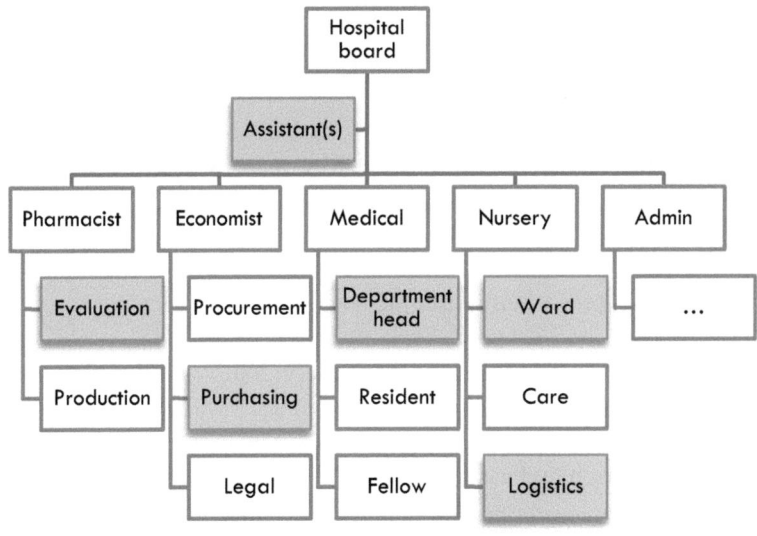

**EXHIBIT 33: ORG CHART - DMU**

Remember the automotive example, in which we indicated 10 different functions, playing a role on your way to achieving the objective.

Some of this research can be done as desk-work. The internet provides many sources of wisdom and there is information you can buy from third parties. Other bits and pieces need personal contact. In this context, it must be clear that confidential information must be kept confidential by all means.

---

*Nothing is more harmful to a lasting and robust business relationship, than missing trust.*

---

Information should be recorded and stored in a systematic way, making details available for the Key Account Manager himself and the KAM-team around him.

Step 1 is to elucidate the functions within the account, relative to your company's objective, the portfolio, and why you declared this account being KEY. In addition, your account will display internal services, acting across departments.

Step 2 is to identify those individuals who may be a DMU-member. Their function may be a clue to know. These steps can be done as desktop research.

Below steps need time and individual presence.

Step 3 is on-site work, identifying those individuals who are part of the DMU-network contributing to decisions.

Step 4 is to research and assign a role to each DMU member. The **role** is relative to your company, whereas the **function** is relative to the organization and displayed in the org-chart.

Usually there is a list of words, applied to indicate which role someone plays. Again this only should serve as an example.

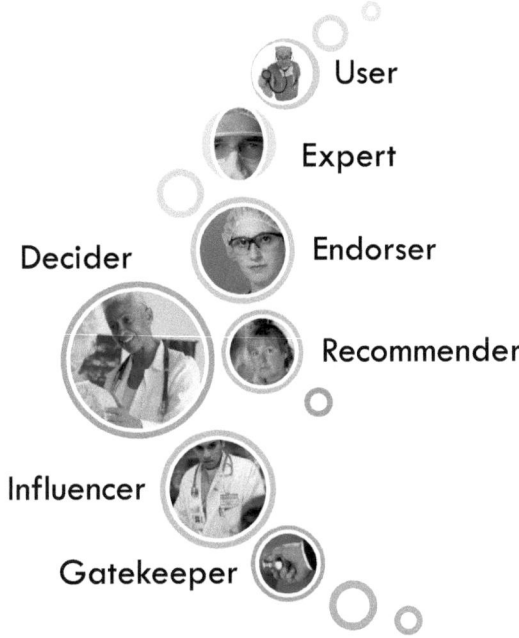

**EXHIBIT 34: DMU-ROLES**

You are well advised to identify and align the roles and your vocabulary to your account-objective. Some explanations of roles, associated with DMU-members and their functions:

- The **Decider** finally signs your proposal.

- **Recommender** is someone, diplomatic enough to make his voice heard, when asked or even when not. He might be the one who opens doors and introduces you.

- The so-called **Endorser** in many companies is a person of high rank, suggesting signing the final contract.

- An **Expert** is an individual whose judgment about a treatment option or any other product or service is internally valued.

- **Users** are those who apply, prescribe or literally use your offering. They are the ones playing a crucial role for "consumption".

- **Influencers** often play a role more in the background. Good if he or she is on your side.

- **Gatekeepers** you will find in any organization. These people often show little involvement in your subject. They simply tend to keep doors as close as possible. This might be the assistant of a senior person or someone with a corporate function in a hospital- or pharmacy-chain.

One of the topics relevant for the professional execution of Key Account Management is documentation. As mentioned earlier you only will learn from failure and be able to improve steps and details, once you document / store them in a structured way.

Remark: only very few CRM-systems allow you to draw an organization-chart, to show the connections of people, even across accounts.

The Gartner-Group recommends: *Do not select vendors solely because they are Leaders in a Magic Quadrant. Often, the most suitable solution is from a Challenger, Visionary or Niche Player.*[46]

---

[46] www.Interactivemedica.com

Documentation of this kind is the domain of few KAM-tools. Problems will start when you try to store an organization-chart or even a network like the DMU with its people and their dependencies. In a complex world some DMU-members might even be located in several accounts and carry a similar role elsewhere.

The detection of all those who are involved in decision-making is the pivotal task for a KEY Account Manager. Once you know who they are, you must find out which role they play.

Knowing the individuals being part of the Decision Making Unit (DMU) is prerequisite for success. Knowing the DMU members and be known by them will establish a valuable competitive advantage.

**Isolate the problem**

Below assumptions or working hypothesis play an important role in professional Key Account Management:

Assumption 1:

Whenever a problem occurs in the $21^{st}$ century, often you will find a solution by yourself. The solution often is not further away, than the next internet search engine.

Consequence: Trying to sell a product will not add any value. Offering a specifically designed solution will make a difference.

Assumption 2:

Many healthcare organizations have specific problems, which are not even properly identified. People inside the account are somewhat unaware of critical issues since their perspective is biased.

Such not-yet-identified issues offer huge opportunities for Key Account Managers dedicated to "go beyond the pill". Detecting and describing a problem will really add value.

Assumption 3:

No one has more knowledge and expertise about a specific disease or condition and other aspects of healthcare, than the related pharmaceutical company. The problem often is that this huge expertise lies in research and development, medical, or market access departments. Knowledge and expertise, related skills, and experiences display a huge, yet untapped treasure hidden in the pharmaceutical industry.

Assumption 4:

No patient will remain untreated when your product is missing. Identifying and offering a solution will deliver a lot more value to an account than simply offering a drug. Responsible as a KAM, you will share the privilege of any other external consultant: the "helicopter view". A perspective from above showing an overview.

This eagle's overview paired with experience from other healthcare providing entities, allows and supports to identify and isolate the account's problems.

**Analytics**

The first step of analysis lead to the fact that the account was identified as KEY account.

With reference to your offering, you know facts and have insight into the economic situation inside the account. For publicly listed companies there are publicly available data. In any other case, the balance sheet might be available elsewhere, structures are displayed in the Internet or inside the account, and people involved can be spotted and identified in places like Facebook, LinkedIn etc. A big proportion of analytics will depend on a KAM's natural curiosity, personal relationships and real-life contacts.

The account objective determines the direction and depth of your analysis. At any step, please consider that analysis only matters, if it helps you taking action. Respecting this, will prevent **paralysis by analysis**.

> Example: Half of the hospitals in Germany are writing red numbers: they spend more money than they make.
>
> If 50% are economically under-performing, 50% must be ok and profitable.
>
> Who is better at finding good examples, network the right people and find a solution for the underperforming hospitals, than a Key Account Manager?

Some more examples for "pain points" or usually unaddressed issues for various kinds of accounts:

- Missing drug adherence of patients is a universal issue, not yet solved and often neglected.

- mHealth, eHealth or Telehealth applications to save time, increase productivity, and assist patients remotely, are subjects of high interest.

- "Patient satisfaction" and loyalty tools like NPS[47] are issues for hospitals and other healthcare providers allowing them to improve reputation and learn from their patients. Not even thought of.

- Leveraging IT tools often is underdeveloped and medical personal wastes huge shares of their time for administration on paper.

- Direct to patient delivery is a differentiator for distributors and pharma companies bringing convenience from FMCG[48] to healthcare - if allowed by regulatory.

- The introduction, maintaining and cultivating "category management" in pharmacies is a great task for wholesalers.

- Asking patients for their experience "and meaning it", is a hot topic for payer organizations.
  ..... be creative and find more.

---

[47] Net Promoter Score®
[48] Fast Moving Consumer Goods

## Set DMU-objective

Identifying and wording an objective in general can be seen as an art.

Coherence and consistency make the real difference. Meeting both will make sure that anybody involved will pull the same rope at the same end and into the same direction.

**EXHIBIT 35: FLOW TO DERIVE STRATEGY FROM OBJECTIVE**

Above graph indicates the necessity and the effect of coherence across the "chain of command". The interrelation of objective and strategy are clear: each level's objective is developed from the strategy above.

Setting a DMU-objective therefore must fully connect and comply with the overriding account objective. The DMU objective will have to show coherence, interrelation, and consistency with the Individual Account Objective. On the other hand, a Key Account Manager's objective follows the same logic.

Account Objective - example:
*"We want to establish collaboration as provider of medical and therapeutical expertise in our areas for this <u>hospital</u>."*

Related DMU objective:
*"We want to make sure that our offering is applied in 35% of all relevant procedures in this <u>hospital</u>. The date of achievement is planned for end of next year."*

Account Objective - example:
*We will approach the <u>payer-organization</u> to convey the outcome value of our offerings for their insured and patients.*

Related DMU objective:
*Within the next 12 months we will try to achieve that for this <u>payer-organization</u> and patients our offering will be the most recommended treatment option.*

Account Objective - example:
*We will optimally support the <u>wholesaler's</u> collaboration with pharmacies and other customers.*

Related DMU objective:
*We will make sure, that our product is recommended to be dispensed during any pharmacy contact made by the <u>wholesaler</u>.*

**DMU-strategy**

Remember: Strategy is the answer to the question: *"How will we achieve the objective?"*

Example objective, copied from above:

> *"We want to make sure that our offering is applied in 35% of all relevant procedures in this <u>hospital</u>. The date of achievement is planned for end of next year."*

The challenge now is to sit down, design, and develop finely honed ways and means to achieve this.

FOOD FOR THOUGHT

> *Ask the chief surgeon for permission to be a visiting observer and record small videos how he applies your product. The videos will be shared with other surgeons through non-public YouTube.*
>
> *or*
>
> *Assist the economic hospital director writing a presentation about the return of investment / cost-benefit relation of alternative procedures as a case study.*

## Design your offering

Above strategies are the outcome of analysis and inspiration that their surgical procedures could be updated.

The answers to the question "how to ..." depend on the issue detected. They will also depend on the degree of creativity that KAMs show and unleash in their KAM team.

**Below quotes indicate that the step of designing appropriate solutions could be the real key to success. At the end and as a resultant, successful projects cause revenue.**

*.... The opportunity is to create a win-win: Create something that is right for the consumer and by doing this, transform a category and create a long-term sustainable growth opportunity for the company.* (Stacy, 2014)

In an article with the title "The Strategy That Will Fix Health Care" written by Michael E. Porter and Thomas H. Lee you will not only find below sentence, but a huge variety of evident issues in healthcare. Most of them appear unknown or pushed aside and neglected.

*Provider organizations understand that, without a change in their model of doing business, they can only hope to be the last iceberg to melt.* (Porter & Lee, 2013)

It is fair to say, that a research-based company owns the largest available insight and expertise in a specific disease area. There are a number of examples for novel approaches and solutions, indicating where the future business model for a pharmaceutical company may lie.

According to CNBC-TV18, an alliance, between a pharmaceutical company and a hospital group, is going to set-up 100 diabetes clinics in India[49]. One of the partners knows everything about running hospitals. The pharma partner knows everything about diabetes.

A government in an emerging market was looking for the best possible Enterprise Resource Planning (ERP) software for their public hospitals. A pharmaceutical KAM heard about their plans and successfully requested support from his colleagues in mature markets. In a fast and efficient international effort, the pharma company requested information from a number of hospitals. They asked users and senior management for their opinion. At the end, the pharmaceutical company introduced the Chief Information Officer (CIO) from a western hospital group and the responsible KAM / project manager of the ERP-provider to the government in the emerging market. Since the pharmaceutical company helped to solve a major problem for the government, they have a significantly high status as the provider of choice in all country's public hospitals.

- Secondary adherence to therapy in asthma symptom control is one of the lowest. It ranges between 7% and around 21% of patients, regularly taking their medication. (Thomas Forissier,

---

[49] https://economictimes.indiatimes.com

2012). In addition, the separation of Rx and OTC business lines mostly prevents contact to pharmacists. A pharmaceutical company designed and implemented a way to pay a reasonable fee to pharmacists for consulting patients how to use their inhalation device. A standardized form needs to be filled and the barcode scanned. This induces payment to the pharmacist. The problem of poor patient outcome for the pneumo-clinic was solved.

- Patients with COPD will start telemonitoring via tablet/mobile devices at their homes that enable them to maintain contact with specialist nurses, in order to enhance their care and avoiding the need for travel. (Wells, 2014)

- A pharma diabetes company has teamed up with several NHS hospitals and a university to provide an integrated care service for people with diabetes. The company will work with King's College London and Guy's and St Thomas', King's College Hospital and South London and Maudsley NHS Foundation Trusts – collectively known as King's Health Partners – to develop a new model of specialist diabetes care in one of the most deprived parts of the UK. Known as i3-diabetes, the five-year programme is a response to the changing role of diabetes care and will aim to integrate specialist services with community and primary care. (Meek, 2014)

Evidently there are huge gaps between patients and healthcare providers in the area of mobile health (mHealth). Many other applications based on current technology are waiting to be closed.

Pharma has yet to establish a sound understanding of possible interactions, the problems that can be solved and the value delivered by leveraging this already far advanced technology.

Which pharmaceutical company is going to team up with Google and their contact lens?

*"Their contact lens uses processing chips and a glucose sensor that have been specially miniaturized for the task, so small that they look like flakes of glitter. Next to them lies an antenna thinner than a human hair. The sensor detects glucose levels in the wearer's tears, taking readings once per second, and the antenna transmits its findings to an external device. This bionic sensor could make a real difference in quality-of-life for diabetics, who have to monitor their blood sugar levels throughout the day."* (Barclay, 2014)

There might be one pivotal prerequisite for such fascinating approaches:

Pharma must develop trust, and one of the ways doing so is to stop "selling drugs" and replace merely "making money", with adding value playing an active role in the delivery of healthcare. Below quote perfectly fits the necessary mind-set for Key Account Management.

*"Programs that transform take patience. Speed to market, probability of quick return, and profitability mind-set have to take a backseat to truly delivering a product that delights the consumer in* **every** *aspect."* (Stacy, 2014)

## Plan activities

Next step is to plan activities. It sounds simple but needs a number of considerations. Each DMU member's needs and their individual requirements are an important starting point.

### Example for a planning exercise

The head of a famous and important university hospital's pharmacy refused to talk about a major pharmacological subject with the KAM. The reason was that the KAM was not a pharmacist himself. Knowing about the importance of this hospital in the country, the pharmacological director insisted to discuss the subject only with the board member responsible for pharmaceutical production.

This request is a hint what the word "management" in KAM stands for: The KAM needs to manage, that the board member will agree to meet the pharmacist, arrange the meeting, run the briefing-session, introduce the two and minute the outcome.

### PLANNING

Planning has both internal and external implications. Planning internally is more about managerial skills.

1.  Internal planning usually starts with identifying the colleagues whom you need as subject matter experts to meet their counterparts in the DMU.

2.  All the members of the KAM-Team need briefing and access to the KAM-tool containing detailed information.
    On the other hand, they will have to share their information, steps and actions. This allows the whole KAM-team to prevent uncomfortable surprises.

3.  If your offering reaches "beyond the pill", your offering must be planned in detail and thoroughly checked for repercussions

in- and outside the account. "What will the general public think of it?" shall be a relevant question.

4.  If your offering does not reach further than one of your products, you still need to plan the details around prices, rebates, logistics etc.

Creative add-ons to reduce pressure on prices by creating a bundle for negotiation could be something as simple as improved logistics: delivering directly to the ward, instead only to the pharmacy or the front door.

1.  Identify who of the KAM-team needs to meet whom.

2.  Plan the content to be discussed with each DMU-member

3.  Make and agree appointments.

4.  The KAM should be present at any of these meeting. The personal introduction of the dialogue partners is a must. It is advisable that the KAM offers to minute meeting results.

**EXHIBIT 36: KAM BRIEFING FLOW**

5.  You need to make sure, that all KAM-team members are carefully briefed. Briefing means details like the subject itself, the reason why to meet, the "pain-point" of the counterpart, the product, the possible value of the lead and so on.

6. Arranging dates and filling agendas on both ends: in the account and internally. It is highly advisable to leverage technology when searching for multilateral facetime. Using www.doodle.com is a pretty popular way doing so.

7. Someone needs to be in charge of preparing travel and booking accommodation etc.

## Execute the plan

Visibility of Key Account Managers in the own organization is high. They carry responsibility for large proportions of the business and their contribution is of major importance.

Execution of any planned activity will be widely registered, followed-up and acknowledged.

Doing what was planned and carefully documenting any deviation is essential to the job of Key Account Manager. Only documentation will allow gap analysis and improvement over time.

## Record activities

While maintaining a business relationship any activity must be recorded. The content should be available to all those who might have contact to the respective DMU-member. An unprepared contact shall be avoided.

> Be aware, that no one has contact with an *account*. Contacts only happen between individuals. Any individual contact, be it by phone, e-mail or personal, should be recorded.

In any case: confidential information is confidential. But the time, the channel, the topic, any agreement made, constitute a mandatory entry into the database. Entries must be made immediately after, if not during the contact. The earlier, the less bias.

On the other hand, anyone inside the company, who is about to contact an individual in an account, must check with the KAM or CRM-tool before he or she establishes a contact. Professional preparation means to look through the contact history and identify the necessary pieces of information. It is unacceptable that anyone from inside the company has a contact with a stakeholder outside and does not know with whom, about what, or when the previous contact had been.

> Remember:
> Any individual DMU-Member can be part of more than one Decision Making Unit. This means that your colleague in a different part of the country probably will contact the same person.

## Monitor achievements and other outcome

Life rarely allows us to fully accomplish what we planned or intended to achieve. Very often, we cover distances in smaller steps than envisioned. Therefore, it is important to record and monitor every bit of achievement, even if it is a small step. Precise and detailed monitoring will indicate if you still are on track, pursuing the same objective, and following your original strategy. As rare as real Key Account Management is, are the tools supporting KAM to the extent necessary.

*"A single, cloud-based application across not just the KAM module but also CRM, Key Opinion Leader management, Launch Optimizer, Campaign Management, Territory Planner, analytics and embedded coaching capability."* [50]

Monitoring is done in a tool, allowing to enter the degree of achievement or result. This may well be a percentage of the original objective. Space must be available for full text entries. The latter will allow the KAM-Team to identify the necessary details about what was missing and probably why.

Trying to figure out in detail, why a planned objective was missed, the so-called fishbone analysis can be helpful. The KAM-Team sits together and tries to brainstorm the central factors for a known or identified shortcoming. After this, you collect possible causes. At the end, you interpret the findings of the team, draw conclusions and make decisions.

The fishbone analysis has its name from the form of a fish's skeleton.

---

[50] Gartner Report 2012, Cool Vendor:
https://wilmingtonhealthcare.com/what-we-do/interactive-medica/

You can easily perform this on a sheet of paper or flipchart, starting at the left.

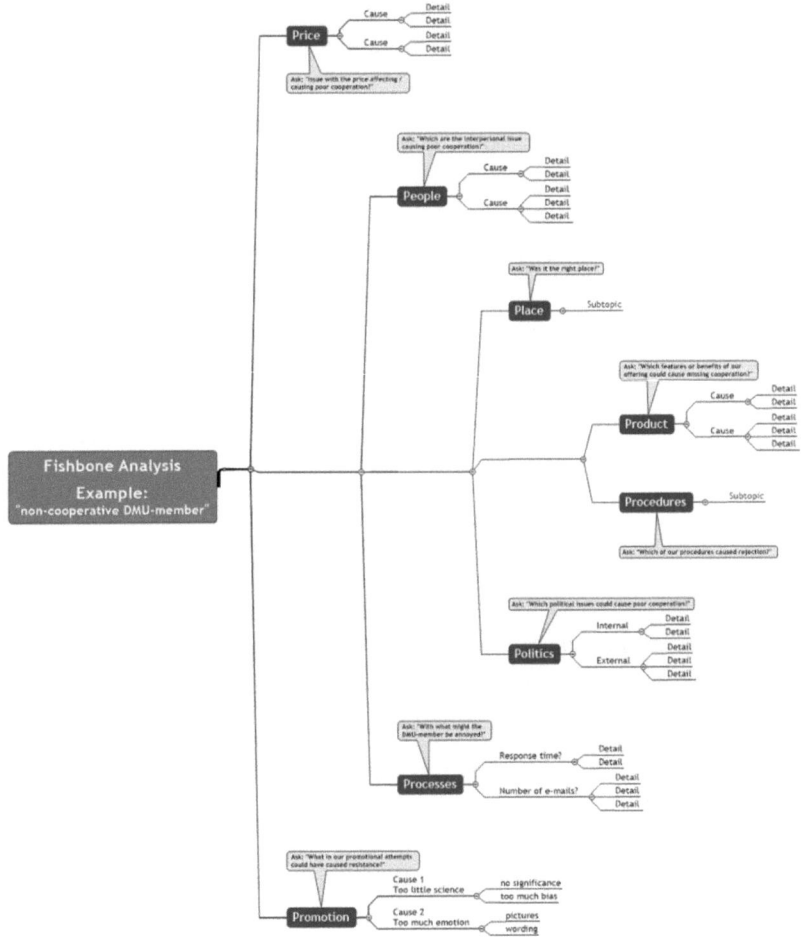

Below steps stand for an appropriate analytical process:

1. Identify the problem
   The problem in the example is stated in the starting box left and here is worded as "non-cooperative DMU member."

2. Identify the "major factors" or issues. The descriptive example uses the 7P's of marketing, as guidance for "major factors."

3. For each factor, you need to identify one or more possible causes. If you bump into another major issue while discussing, declare this a "major factor" and put it at the appropriate level.

The fish-bone diagram will then be ready and can be filled with relevant content.

4. The last step is to interpret the diagram and draw conclusions. If you do not find a major cause, drive your analysis deeper.

Imagine the major reason for an uncooperative DMU-Member would be an interpersonal problem due to incompatible personalities? Once identified, a solution in this specific case could be to assign someone else from the KAM-team to take over and bring the contact to fruition.

**Ensure continuity**

Key Account Management has little to do with fast cash business harvesting "low hanging fruits". The concept itself is about lasting and robust business relationships. Very normally, flows and processes take their time, but at the end will be ever more rewarding. A key account and its DMU-members deserve attention. There is plenty of room, opportunity, and necessity to keep individual relations alive.

# CULTURE & MIND-SET

Mind-set is step number three of an important managerial triple jump, consisting of

1. Structures

2. Processes

3. Mind-set

*Any structure should follow strategy.* (Mauborgne & Kim, 2009)

It might help to improve the understanding of *mind-set*, assuming that etymologically the word comes from "setting your mind". This usually refers to a mind-setting event. This must not be traumatic but must be deep enough to trigger a change in your mind-set.

A company needs to go a number of steps, before the transformation to Key Account Management will be achieved. Remember that KAM is not just another sales technique. Revenue and achieving business numbers will "only" be a resultant of your efforts.

# DRIVERS OF MIND-SET

Four company categories, named to the point by Rubicon, inspired below flow. The naming of the categories indicates the changes in the structures, processes and mind-set on the way to becoming a KAM-organization. (Rubicon, 2014)

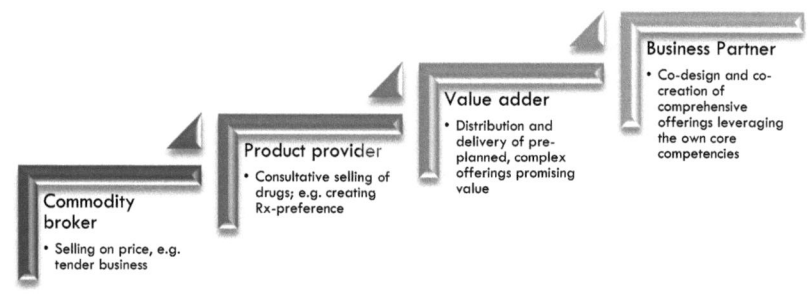

**EXHIBIT 37: PATHWAY TO KAM**

## Commodity broker

In the 21st century, being a "commodity broker" could still be a valuable and valid business model. Selling non-branded, INN generics still does create a decent top, but a poorer bottom line.

The market of non-branded generics in most places is driven by "best price". If any other differentiator is missing, this market segment will end in an oligopolistic setting, with very few, if any, niches.

It is hard to imagine that producers in central Europe and other mature markets can possibly produce and deliver their drugs reasonably cheap, compared to the huge markets and players in China and India.

Field forces are becoming obsolete over time, because there is no room for any field-force influence left.

Few Key Account Managers will establish and run this commodity business. They will help procurement and logistics on the account side, and fight for reduced prices internally.

Tenders will drive this part of the drug business on the demand side. Commodity suppliers develop and follow a price-leadership strategy.

The word price-"leadership" indicates and implies that, in theory, "there can only be one". Looking into examples in any other market, the survival rate in price leadership strategies is small.

In any case, even this business model will only work with human (inter-) faces = Key Account Managers.

**Product provider**

There is a gap between the view of the pharmaceutical industry and payers or physicians about the degree of innovativeness and adding therapeutic value of products. In any case novel compounds need consultation and information transfer. If pharma manages to narrow or close the gap in perception, it is fine.

Foreseeably more products will be denied the status of "being better than the current standard therapy" by those who own the budgets.

There are a number of innovative drugs like DDP4-antagonists and even biologicals with similar or the same indication, which may fall into this category.

Product providers need the consulting role of medical reps. Their number was significantly reduced in the past years. Despite this reduction, accessibility to physicians in the US is at an all-time low. Medical representatives can visit only 51% of physicians in the US in 2014.

*"Doctors continue to turn away from face-to-face visits from pharma sales reps and look instead towards mobile technology for information."* (Tyer & Pickering, 2014)

In Australia, a campaign has even been started in 2014 with the title: "Free yourself from drug reps".[51]

There are strong indicators that doctors deny offering 1 to 5 minutes contact time. Most probably because these few minutes do not add any value to their professional every-day life.

Products will be promoted(?) to prescribers and users by guidelines, medical literature, expert advice, non-pharma websites, demanding patients and other sources. The "product providing industry" will be denied to play a major role in promotion. Trends show that even novel compounds or biotech drugs will have two price tags: the official price and a negotiated reimbursement price.

To achieve this, skilled but very few Key Account Managers will be necessary.

**Value Adder**

"Adding value", "value adding" or "added value" are frequently used, yet undefined terms.

Probably we disagree that below economical definition indicates what you mean with "adding value"?

*In economics, the sum of the unit profit, the unit depreciation cost, and the unit labor cost is the unit value added. Summing value added per unit over all units sold is total value added. Total value added is*

---

[51] http://www.noadvertisingplease.com/

*equivalent to revenue less outside purchases (of materials and services).[52]*

Some people in pharma still believe a patient brochure will add value to a healthcare provider. Others already find that patient education is adding value and others are trying to provide apps next to their drug.

In most cases, those added-value services are free, and their aim to increase revenue of pharma is very or better too evident, superficial and perceived as not adding value to the HCP community.

The 1,000 $ question is "Is pharma ready to get here?":

*Any definition of value in healthcare must align with the "triple aim"—to improve population outcomes and enhance quality of life while simultaneously lowering healthcare costs.* (Quintiles, Value is the target, 2014)

Seriously considering exactly this, can pave the way for pharma or medtech companies, towards becoming a business partner to healthcare providers.

## Business Partner / KAM

There is constant exchange of value, service, or products for money in healthcare. Imaging in many mature markets the healthcare arena contributes more than 10% to a nation's Gross Domestic Product.

Undoubtedly, healthcare at any level is a huge and growing business. The big difference between pharma and healthcare companies is, that the central objective in healthcare is not making money. Healthcare providers are not measured by "revenue achieved".

---

[52] http://en.wikipedia.org/wiki/Value_added

It is patient outcome and quality of care, which is a central goal.

If you have a look at automotive you will see blueprints for pharma developing and moving towards "business partnership" = KAM:

Component suppliers of car manufactures share joint teams of engineers with their client companies, they share offices and computer networks. Component supplying companies physically surround plants of their manufacturers. Delivering the optimal service fully integrated into the value-chain of the manufacturer and the shortest possible way for their contribution and products is their dedication.

Key Account Managers of FMCG companies often have an office within their client company. In regular meetings within their client companies, they pursue their common and mutual business objective: make the consumer happy and as a consequence or resultant, generate growth, market share and additional revenue.

These examples should shed more light what Key Account Management could mean for pharma.

# CULTURE EATS STRATEGY FOR BREAKFAST

The sentence *"Culture eats strategy for breakfast."* is attributed to Peter Drucker, the highest reputed and the most famous management teacher of the 20th century. Drucker's sentence contains a very clear message: The way from being a "commodity provider" to professional Key Account Management is long and full of hardships and needs a new culture triggered by changes in mind-set.

It not only needs appropriate structures fully supporting the new business model. It needs shift and cultural change from *selling drugs* to *playing an active role in healthcare.*

## Structures

Changing company structures needs comparatively little effort. You call a consulting firm, and they will do what they did with many others: They will tell you about the so-called "benchmarks" and "best practices" and advise you to do the same as the others.[53]

If you want to be brighter than others, you use the term "restructuring" for what it means: it is about defining and deploying novel or changed structures in the company or part of it. Once you have defined the new structures, HR and management will announce and implement the new organization chart with solid and dotted lines. Easy. SAP or other ERP-software will then have to be up-dated with the new structures. Although often perceived as such, *restructuring* itself does not mean a simplistic reduction of headcount.

---

[53] Example taken from experience

Consultant's next business is to redefine high level business processes to align them with the new structure.

Provocatively worded, the very common outcome of such costly exercise is that the time for meetings and face-to-face discussions will multiply, and new managers will have different assessments of their people. The disruption will be significant and usually company results and employees will suffer.

In the 21$^{st}$ century employees no longer are willing to suffer. The key people and high performers often leave the company as early as they detect the first consultants on site. Finding a new employer is generally easy for the top 20%. It is a predictable loss for the current employer. Losing the best talent is a consequence and should be foreseeable.

## Processes

Business processes usually are renovated at high level. This again will allow older and traditional processes being kept alive. The only difference is that they are no longer happening next door or next desk, but probably in the cafeteria or at lunch. Undoubtedly, structures and processes need to be updated and changed to achieve the next level. Any change, the next step on the ladder, can only be achieved, if culture and mind-set share the same attention and investment, as structure and processes.

## Changing culture

Considering an individual person, any change of habits and mind-set is disruptive by nature. John P. Kotter[54] is the world's leading expert on change. He found that around 70% of all major change projects fail.

---

[54] The 8-Step Process for Leading Change | Dr. John Kotter (kotterinc.com)

The journey from being a value adding company to become a Business Partner in healthcare is a change project of considerable dimension. If you want to be part of the winning 30%, you are well advised to apply the "rules of change", established by John P. Kotter. (Kotter, John P., 2014)

1. Establishing a Sense of Urgency

2. Build a Guiding Coalition

3. Form a Strategic Vision and Initiatives

4. Enlist a volunteer army

5. Enable action by removing barriers

6. Generate short-term wins

7. Sustain acceleration

8. Institute change

*Most major change initiatives—whether intended to boost quality, improve culture, or reverse a corporate death spiral, generate only lukewarm results. Many fail miserably.* (Kotter, Leading Change - Why transformation efforts fail, 2003)

Professionally managing change is a key driver within the attempt to becoming a business partner and successfully implement KAM.

Most academic details and findings around managing change reflect a simple aspect:

- Every one of us will only change habits and mind-set, if there is a reason to do so.

- The reason to change must come out of ourselves and must have its origin in insight. It will hardly be possible to talk or "powerpoint" people into changing habits and mind-set. Change can be triggered by a related event.

- If training, presentations, lectures, or other internal communication miss to create this *sense of urgency*, you will lose the case.

- There is plenty of literature dealing with change and yet again: there is not "one size fitting all".

- Beware of standard-, off-the-shelf solutions.

## Culture or Mind-set

Culture is the final step of change. Culture in this context is well defined with below sentence:

> *"Culture is the pattern of behaviors and beliefs characteristic to a social group, in this case a company.*

If you want to get a very first idea about aspects of company culture, carefully read your or other's display panels in the lobby, directed to employees. If you ever read something similar to this, it will tell you a lot: *"This is the final reminder that your guests have to stay away from the executive's parking lots!"*

There are several aspects around company culture, referring more to patterns of behavior: *"I will not make myself redundant giving away my know-how!?"* or *"This is marketing and I am in sales!"* or *"My MSL[55]s cannot support any kind of commercial activity."*

There are a number of details in KAM, which need a specific culture and mind-set. One of the top issues is cross-functional cooperation. Anyone can easily imagine the difficulty trying to embed KAM in a departmental culture. Remember: the word "department" is derived from Latin: *departire*. This means division, dividing, divorce, or (de)parting. The word itself has nothing to do with *cooperation*. It sends a respective signal. Working together is vitally necessary on your way to KAM. Probably some thoughtful people in earlier days saw this as well and invented the word "business unit". Remember: this word was invented and introduced on purpose. It was meant to deploy cultural change and get rid of "departmental walls". Closely related to culture is the mind-set.

Again, there is a very plausible definition or meaning of mind-set. Etymology explains the part "set": *it indicates that the mind has been set by an experience or event.*

*"Habits of mind formed by previous experience," in educators' jargon, from mind (n.) + set* (Etymonline, 2014)

Often heard words like *client centricity*, *values*, and *trust* are supposed to reflect mind-sets, which can play a major role when starting or continuing the KAM-journey.

*"The pharma industry is well positioned to deliver so much more value to healthcare, beyond providing pills and vaccines, but it will require a significant change in mind-set and intent. The days of seeing the pill as the value the industry provides is gone, stakeholders are demanding*

---

[55] Medical Science Liaison

*more from pharma than ever before"* (David Laws, @eyeforpharma, 2014).

# MEASURES AND METRICS

When matching above quote from David Laws with the sentence "Everything you do and say sends a signal", attributed to Philip Kotler, you can see where the problem lies: the signals the industry sends are displaying and rightfully perceived as a profit-driven mind-set.

It does not matter at all, if the industry sends this message unintentionally, grossly negligent or on purpose. The message perceived by stakeholders and anyone else, is about top- and bottom-line. The pharmaceutical industry is perceived as being driven by revenue and profit (only).

Senior managers evidently close their eyes and do not see the far-reaching implication of what is measured within their company. Everyone pretends to know the famous quote assigned to William Hewlett: *"You only can manage what you measure."* and the addendum almost is a business mantra in these days: *"What you measure gets done!"*

Both of these sentences reflect the very normal human strive and search for harmony. *"They measure this item because this appears to be important for them. Consequently, I will act accordingly".*

Assumedly there is more than a <u>correlation</u> between measures and how people act. Measures seem to be a major <u>cause</u> for problems, and this does not only apply to pharma. In Harvard Business Review, Steve Kerr commented the huge problems General Motors faced in 2014 around ignition-switch defects:

*"Although managers' bonuses are based partly on vehicle-quality improvements, and safety is supposed to be paramount, cost is "everything" at GM, and the company's atmosphere probably*

*discouraged individuals from raising safety concerns."* (Steve Kerr, HBR, 2014)

Another quite funny example is when traffic congestion did not allow bus drivers to be in time. To resolve the issue of missing schedule, bus drivers haven been measured by punctuality. Bonus payments have been promised depending on punctuality. What happened? They did not stop at most bus-stops any longer to be in time at those measured.

The hypothesis one can draw out of this: It is not (only) bonuses driving actions and mind-set, but already "What you measure gets done." In any case, this sounds and appears plausible, and experience backs this assumption widely.

David Law's sentence about the *"significant change in mind-set and intent"* really should propel the adoption of novel and different metrics and measures in pharma. If pharma appears to be solely affixed and focused on *sales* or *revenue*, the industry cannot live up to all their lip-service of customer- or patient centricity.

**Units of Measurement / Metrics**

To be clear with the vocabulary, there are two terms of interest: measures and metrics. Definition: if you want to *measure* the speed of a car, you need time and way as *metrics*.

$$\frac{distance}{time} = km/hour$$

Traditionally pharma measures sales and their equivalents like growth or market share and attribute them to their medical reps. They do this, neglecting the fact that a medical the medical reps hardly have an influence. They cannot "create" additional patients, and they hardly can change therapeutic habits of more than few prescribers. How and why sales are measured, depends on several aspects and cultural backgrounds.

Some quotes might sound familiar:

"We pay small salaries and high bonus to keep our sales-people hungry!"

"Our reps are fully motivated by their sales targets and the related bonus."

"The highest market share wins!"

"Our bonus system is designed that 25% of our reps do not get bonus."

….

Measuring "sales" is done in many ways. Revenue achieved is only one parameter. Revenue measured in an ATC (therapeutic class) ends up with market share. Market share of territories compared to the country's market share delivers you the market share index. The number of variations is numerous and in any case drives and determines the company culture, the prevailing mind-set, and the subsequent actions of individuals.

If *"everything you do and say, sends a signal"*, above examples point to a "very special" company culture.

Additionally, the underlying assumption, that money motivates, is *"more folklore than science"*. (Dan Pink, 2014)

There is plenty of research and a lot of literature about the widely inexistent motivational power of money. Dan Pink is one of the authors worthwhile to watch on YouTube®. "The Puzzle of Motivation" is one of his masterpieces.

**Remark:**

Any enterprise needs sales and other external, leading and lagging indicators along the Profit & Loss statement or the Balance Sheet.

> The problem lies in the fact that many of these figures are "resultants" of efforts. They hardly are parameters, which you can directly influence. Generating *revenue* is not within your arm's length.

> Consequently, it is a rather critical exercise to hold someone responsible for "sales". Creating sales-targets means to pretend you can manage sales. You cannot.

> There is no immediate impact of any managerial action reaching out into the market towards contracts signed, products prescribed etc.

You easily can manage the number of calls made by your field-force. You only need to tell them. Trying to do this with "sales" will prove that management's arm is too short.

> Sales or revenue are vitally important "business figures". They should not be misused or misunderstood as objectives in the context of MbO.[56]

No one will ever neglect that any enterprise's "raison d'etre" is to make money and being a business. The question is if "making money" can

---

[56] Management by Objective

be an objective or if it is not a lot better to see *revenue* as a planned figure, pouring in as a *resultant* of all your company's and colleagues' efforts.

Measures and their metrics must definitely be established to reflect the purpose and the intention of Key Account Management.

**Appropriate measures**

In the Eyeforpharma's Industry Healthcheck 2014 there is a remarkable headline saying that *"73% [of pharma managers] agree that pharma companies need to become genuine healthcare providers."*

David Laws comments this statement with:

*"Another example that pharma knows what needs to be done but is unable or unwilling to execute beyond pilots and tests. They clearly do not yet see a financial advantage in moving in this direction."* (David Laws, @eyeforpharma, 2014)

The matching counterpart to David Law's statement is the sentence: *"As long as pharma is affixed to setting sales targets to their people, pharma will remain unable to become customer- or even patient-centric."*

Experience and observation us that the sentence "What you measure gets done." is true in all consequence. To make patient centricity happen and drive mind-set in this direction, measuring sales per head is counterproductive. How to identify measures, driving the efforts of an organization into the right direction?

*There is not one "right" direction.*
*There only is your direction!*

This can be a flow assisting to identify "your" direction:

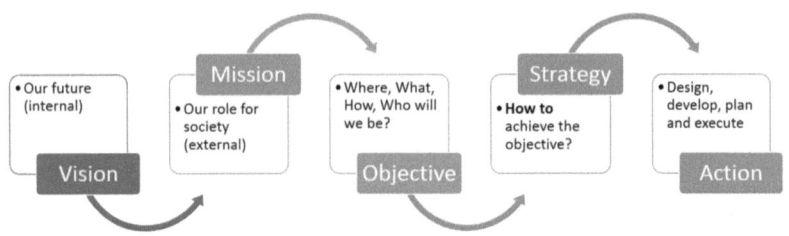

**EXHIBIT 38: GIVING DIRECTION**

Following these steps will allow you to identify the most appropriate units to measure. Measures will indicate where you want to go. In the same instance, measures will show if you still are on the right way to achieve the objective.

SAMPLE SET OF MEASURES

Please note: at this stage questions how to measure or where to get the data from are irrelevant.

If you identify a measure or metric that matches your objective, supports the right mind-set, and assumedly will result in the appropriate actions, and can lead to managerial consequences or actions that matter, you will surely find a way to measure.

*"Sales Data Only Matters If It Helps You Take Action!"* (Andris A. Zoltners, 2014)

Let us take below statement, the "heart of this book" as a mission statement and an example to derive measures:

*Key Account Management is about establishing a lasting and robust business partnership dedicated to improving the delivery of healthcare.*

In this assumed "mission statement", you find several words, which could be the basis for measures in and along Key Account Management

> Remark: As indicated earlier, the word "performance" is undefined. Clarity, meaningfulness and being calculable, rather than fully subjective, are mandatory items for measuring.

Let us take three terms as a basis to identify coherent[57] and consistent[58] units to measure, if you are on the right track to achieve KAM.

1. Lasting

2. Robust

3. Improved delivery of healthcare

EXAMPLES FOR MEASURES INDICATIVE TO *"LASTING"*

1. duration of the business relationship.

2. number of repetitive orders.

3. order frequency

4. order interval

---

[57] Coherence: each step connects to, or follows the other
[58] Consistency: all steps fit together serving the same objective

1. number of people you have regular contact with.

2. lead time necessary to agree on meetings.

3. touch points inside the account you have immediate access to.

4. number of times you are actively asked to come and meet DMU-members.

EXAMPLES FOR MEASURES INDICATIVE TO *IMPROVING DELIVERY OF HEALTHCARE"*

1. number of patients benefitting from our offering.

2. feedback about the perception of our assistance and offering.

3. Net Promoter Score® values.

4. reduction of in-patient treatment time.

5. degree of contribution to improved outcome.

6. ...

For your forecasting, production, supply chain, and business planning you need and have a different set of business figures.

# THE KEY ACCOUNT MANAGER

This chapter tries to give some guidance and food for thought about the individuals being meant by the acronym KAM.

*Key are those accounts, which are of top / key priority and relevance for the company.*

Such an account must be in the hands of a person who meets the standards of DMU-members, fully can master the necessary detail, being persistent and persevering enough to manage the internal KAM-team and being sufficiently resilient to get along with disappointments.

Learning from mistakes and not repeat them is another important trait or characteristic of such a "jack of all trades".

Key Account Managers are the gold reserve of a company. The most important question about finding them is to "make or buy"?

# TEMPTATION OR APPROPRIATE STEP?

*Blow up your sales force... or at least consider it. That's the message today from Deloitte Consulting, which has analyzed pharma sales and come up with some conclusions designed to provoke thought.* (W. Scott Evangelista, Deloitte, 2009)

Many companies and CEOs since then have seen that reducing their field force of medical representatives, calling and detailing doctors, does not really harm top line revenue. It therefore can be a temptation to "make KAMs from reps". Valid step or not is a valid question.

In the past years, many pharmaceutical reps have lost their jobs due to so-called restructurings and the reduction of the number of reps in the field. In some cases, this was a blessing for the bottom-line not even harming the top-line. It is clear and normal that the question pops up: can KAM be a career path for a medical representative? The answer is the one you are used to hear from lawyers: "It depends."

The approach and goal must be clear: you need the best person as a Key Account Manager. The central issue is what does "the best" really mean for your specific company and its current situation. Again: there is not "one size fitting all!"

## Key Account Manager: Make or Buy?

To meet this challenge, you need to know about the important difference between a medical rep and a KAM, getting a very clear idea of your company's KAM-profile.

Below list is descriptive, and there may be differences and details fitting your current situation better. It is worthwhile to collect your own list. Taking the job-description of a rep as a starting point will help.

| A pharmaceutical rep | A Key Account Manager |
|---|---|
| works alone | establishes an internal KAM-Team and manages their contacts inside the account |
| The objective is short term revenue | The objective is to create and maintain a robust and lasting business relationship |
| deals with many physicians | identifies, knows and covers a limited number of contacts in an account: the DMU members |
| leverages individual relationships, to improve prescriptions / sales | develops a deep understanding for his contacts, learns about their needs and requirements, isolates a possible issue and develops an offering meeting their needs and requirements |
| uses the same message with any of his contacts, to achieve his objectives. | is about targeted communication, using many kinds of resources and tools in the effort to meet needs and requirements. |
| visits as many contacts as possible per day. | Face time in the account usually is below 50%. |
| Contacts to be visited are pre-set. | identifies relevant DMU-members himself. |
| is the „only living interface" between the company and the physician. | finds the right counterparts for each DMU-member in his company. |
| details and promotes few and changing products. | identifies solutions drafts and conveys concepts. |
| knows his product and answers specific questions. | identifies therapeutic or other problems, arranges and cares for the best possible person to answer. |

## KAM-Profile

Below example is copy / pasted from a job offering for a Pharma Key Account Manager in the US. When conceptually compared to KAM this list shows several deficits and the company might not mean the Key Account Management concept described in this book.

However, it can serve as guidance indicating how different requirements may be even applying the same term: Key Account Management.

The Key Account Manager ("KAM") is responsible for offering support and assistance of a specific key account. The KAM will ensure coordination and alignment with all functional groups within our company regarding this key account.

Following this job description, the KAM has to cover these three areas of focus:

1. *Effectively communicate appropriate technical, therapeutic, disease state and product information to promote the use of our products.*

2. *Relationship Management with top tier accounts- building relationships with key personnel, advocates/ thought leaders, pharmacy, finance, professional societies, ancillary healthcare providers.*

3. *Promotional programs.*

### *Responsibility:*

- *Execute sales and marketing strategies. Conduct sales calls to oncologists, nurses, fellows, and other key customers consistent with company compliance policies, applicable law and guidance from U.S. Legal Department.*

- *Responsible for coordination of resources such as sales, marketing, access and reimbursement, medical affairs, and operations within key accounts.*

- *Understand the access landscape, establish / expand medical and/or pharmacy coverage, and facilitate pull through with Pharmacy Directors, Clinical Pharmacists, and other key customers.*

- *Deep knowledge of hospital organizational practices including formulary management, provider contracting, utilization review, clinical practice standard development and pharmaceutical product review.*

- *Creates opportunities to leverage and drive commercial success while enhancing our image and commitment to medicine, working directly with Thought Leaders, Professional Societies, and Advocacy Groups.*

- *Provides strategic insight and competitive information to Marketing, Sales, and Medical Affairs.*

- *Identify and communicate field issues, opportunities, and competitive activities through appropriate organizational venues.*

- *Attends and participates in sales meetings, training classes, seminars, conventions, and other business activities.*

- *Identifies opportunities and develops relationships with current and future health care providers in the nursing community.*

This appears more of being more a job-offer for a "super-rep", with the ability to promote, sell, and convince. Key Account Management is different. Someone who is supposed to *"Execute sales and marketing strategies"* is different from what is meant by Key Account Management in this book.

## Characteristics of a Key Account Manager

Some of below words may indicate inherent, non-trainable traits some may be learnable attitudes. The list is sorted alphabetically.

1. Comprehensive skills using state-of-the-art IT-tools

2. Creativity

3. Deep knowledge of the own offering and the company's abilities

4. Emotional intelligence

5. Entrepreneurial objective setting and planning (OKR[59])

6. Insight into the inner processes and procedures in the account

7. Integrity

8. Intense structural knowledge of the account

9. Knowledge and skills to meet DMU-member's expectations

10. Legal compliance

11. Self-motivation and resilience

12. Sense of responsibility

---

[59] Objectives and Key Results
(https://www.atlassian.com/software/confluence/templates/okrs)

You might want to draft your KAM–requirements in a specific order, more detailed, and in categories. Drafting a paper which will serve as a checklist when deciding to whom you want to hand over the full responsibility of one of your key accounts is a good idea anyway.

Your Human Resource people will surely be happy to suggest a fully fletched list of items indicating towards your optimal Key Account Manager.

Once such list is available a related set of questions is needed. This will support professional assessment if the applicant meets the item or not.

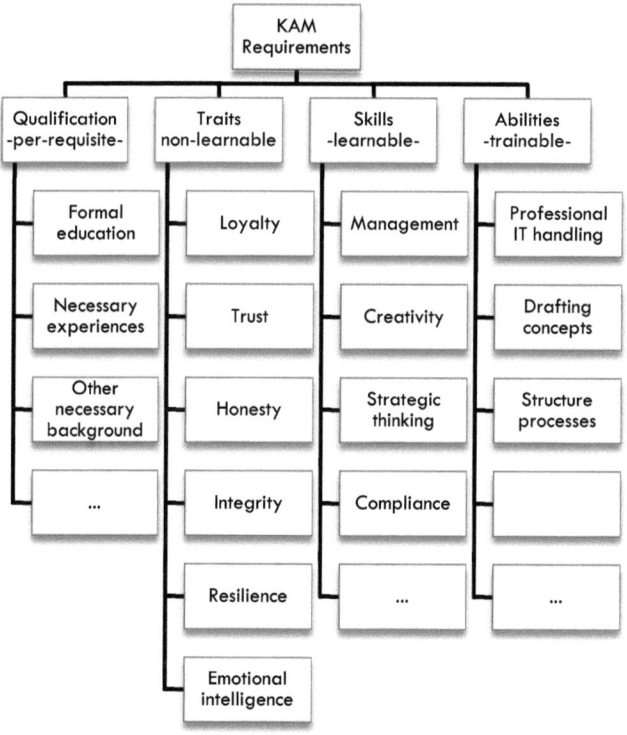

**EXHIBIT 39: LIST OF CATEGORIES / ITEMS**

From experience, a "Yes / No" decision will fully suffice. More details like a scaled answer mostly lead to pseudo-factual decisions and do not add value in the process of identifying the best possible person.

At the end, it does not matter, if you "make or buy" your next KAM. It only must be clear that decision-makers carry far-reaching responsibility, when nominating someone for Key Account Manager.

Detecting the right people can well be supported by a self-assessment of applicants. There is one pre-requisite: every item you ask, must be clear, defined and the criteria fully understood and agreed. Trust them. They know what they do. Below graph is the result of such aself-assessment of three KAMs in the same company.

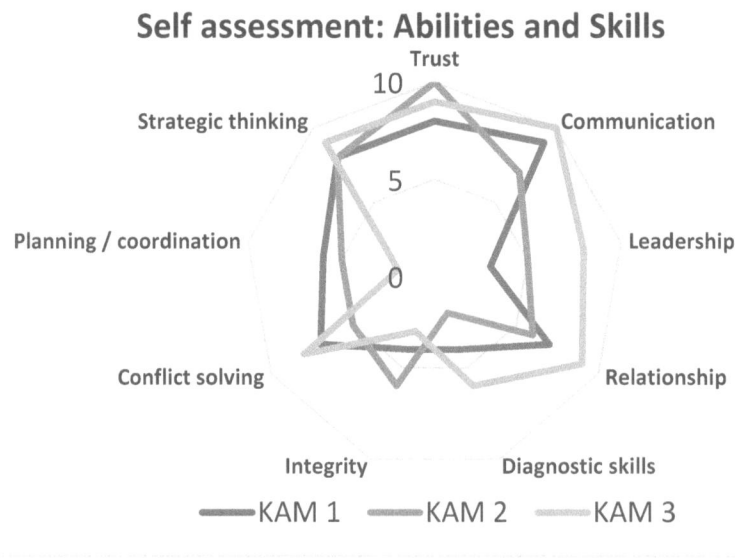

**EXHIBIT 41: SAMPLE FRAMEWORK FOR SELF-ASSESEMENT**

## KAM Job Description

As any other job description, it must contain general tasks and responsibilities of the KAM, to whom the position reports, and other specifications such as skills needed and the degree and limits of the authority to sign contracts on the company's behalf.

These are some suggested details needed both for the organization and for the applicant.

- The KAM's position in the organization chart. This must include solid- and dotted reporting lines.

- The description of the KAM's tasks and scope of job.

- The objective of the KAM-position.

- The space of authority.

- The reporting-requirements.

- Criteria for achievement and success in general.

- …

Feel free to add more detail if appropriate and adds value to your company.

---

*Remember: Details Only Matter If They Help You Take Action.*

---

## KAM remuneration

The reason to insert this remark on Management by Objective, has a lot to do with the remuneration or compensation package for a Key Account Manager.

The habit of setting quarterly sales targets is contradictive to the concept of KAM: *"Establishing and maintaining a robust and lasting business relationship"*.

Remuneration guidelines could be:

1. Fair compensation. Ask yourself, what will happen, if you would make salaries etc. public. Herzberg's hygiene factors serve as valuable hint into the right direction.

2. Compensation must be competitive.
   Believing that saving money on the payroll will be compensated by employer-loyalty will show to be erroneous.

3. Compensation must reward the right behavior.
   What rewarding the wrong behavior means, has become clear in several cases of misconduct. Fines of more than 3 bn US$ paid by pharma companies, indicate the degree of misbehavior driven by wrong metrics and rewards.

4. The regular salary must allow any employee to lead a decent life and match the position.

5. Parts of a compensation package may be "additional".

Salary is regularly paid for an employee's time and effort contributing to the running business. For the employing company, salary is the cost of acquiring and retaining human resources.

Fringe benefits are paid to retain talent or make a company more attractive for new hiring. Additional benefits often charm finance since they might be part of a variable payment scheme.

Bonus and incentives by definition are variable. They are part of many "compensation packages", but only are paid "under the circumstance that …."

Definitions:

> *Bonus* is a variable payment, usually paid once a year, depending on the total performance (of the company)."Performance" mostly equals outcome and results.

> *Incentive* is a financial offer to induce specific patterns of behavior.

Depending how KAMs are positioned in your corporate structure, the compensation package must be thoughtfully designed. KAMs can be high-ranking, reporting directly to the CEO or General Manager. Remember that only very few accounts in a country are key and consequently there will only be few KAMs.

> Example: In a big global European group of companies in the area of investment goods, there are only five global KEY accounts. Each one of them is assigned to a C-level executive. The task is that, in addition to the presence of the KAM, each C-level executive will visit "his" key account once a year.

Considering the business-model of KAM, short term financial or revenue goals or bonuses tied to them, are inappropriate. In KAM the objective of designing a remuneration package should be driven by the strong will to hire the best and keep them as long as possible. A wrong hiring and a premature firing can cost a fortune.

## KAM objective setting

The objectives for a Key Account Manager will follow the mission statement. The co-creation of offerings together with an institution to achieve improved outcome of healthcare will need time. Imagine the timespan needed to gain a contract with a government about building a new power plant. This time is calculated in years. Why should an agreement with a government, about improving healthcare outcome for a specific population, create revenue in the next quarter?

How you set or better agree objectives and which kind of objectives you identify, will be indicative to the degree of maturity of your KAM approach.

A number of misunderstandings around objective setting in conjunction with management by objectives (MbO) is evident:

> Drilling expected or forecasted revenue top-down into a sales and marketing organization is wasting resources and time-consuming. This has not been Peter Drucker's idea when "inventing" *Management by Objective.*

Achieving "sales" or "market share" isn't even in the company's reach and hands, since the "market" happens outside of your company. People, clients, or DMU-members may sign contracts within a reporting period or not. It is fully up to them, to create *your* revenue. Below quote shall shed some light on this objective-setting practice, which assumedly even contradicts the objective to establish a "lasting and robust business relationship" with a Key Account.

*Management by objectives (MBO), also known as management by results (MBR), is a process of defining objectives within an organization so that management and employees agree to the objectives and understand what they need to do in the organization in order to achieve them.* (Wikipedia, 2014)

Two major areas should be underlined:

1. MbO is *a process to agree objectives,* not set them, let alone deal and negotiate them like in a bazar.

2. The other area is that the quote says: "defining objectives within an organization".

When manager and employee start to negotiate expected market figures, be sure there is something going wrong, especially if you want to apply term and principles of "management by objective."

The second major area is indicated by the word "*... process of defining objectives **within** an organization....*"

---

> *MbO identifies and mutually agrees objectives within the organization.*

---

Example: *"Having educated and fully equipped Key Account Managers to have them productively on-board until start of first quarter."* might be a great objective for HR, fully in line with Peter Drucker's concept of MbO. Objectives for a Key Account Manager in the best case should follow the KAM-process. An objective sounding like "Having fully identified and documented all relevant roles and functions in the decision-making-unit by ... ." will meet the standards of MbO.

In the future it will be a much better idea to implement OKR[60] as management principle, especially in Key Account Management. OKR was first rolled-out in Intel and is implemented in a number of high-tech and *agile* companies, like Google, Microsoft, Uber, and Twitter.

---

[60] **O**bjective and **K**ey **R**esults

OKRs comprise an objective, a clearly defined goal and 3–5 key results, specific measures used to track the achievement of that goal. The goal of OKR is to define how to achieve objectives through concrete, specific and measurable actions. Key results can be measured on a 0–100% scale or any numerical unit (e.g. dollar amount, %, items, etc.). Objectives should also be supported by initiatives, which are the plans and activities that help to achieve the objective and move forward the key results. OKRs may be shared across the organization with the intention of providing teams with visibility of goals with the intention to align and focus effort.[61]

OKRs consist of:

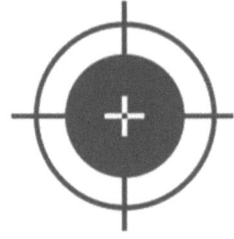

**Objectives**

A statement of a broad goal, usually qualitative in nature.

**Key Results**

A statement that measures achievement of a given objective.

**EXHIBIT 40: OBJECTIVES AND KEY RESULTS**
LICENSED BY CC BY-SA-NC

---

[61] https://en.wikipedia.org/wiki/OKR

# KAM TOOLS

A tool is needed to fulfil a task in the attempt to achieve the intended results. Tools in all regularity have a specific format and are closely tied to and support a specific procedure. In principle, there are two kinds of tools applied in Key Account Management:

1. Electronic tools like ERP[62] and CRM[63]

2. Strategy tools like SWOT and PEST etc.

**Electronic tools:**

Enterprise Resource Planning tools cover the full enterprise including the value chain. They reach from procurement / purchasing, research and development, to production, distribution, accounting, human resources, compliance, governance, to customer services, marketing, and sales. ERP tools are complex. The structures of the majority of pharmaceutical companies still show considerably siloed structures. This is why CIOs[64] often strive, fight, and lose when they want ERP-software to include and cover marketing and sales. The latter two often lead a separate life.

CRM:

**C**ustomer **R**elationship **M**anagement stands both for a mind-set and a piece of software. The most important part of the TLA[65] is the "R" in the middle. Not a software, but something about the interrelation of human beings.

---

[62] Enterprise Resource Planning
[63] Customer Relationship Management
[64] Chief Information Officer (IT)
[65] Three Letter Acronym

Until today CRM-tools for sales and the field-force are often used as policing tool for field forces. Reporting rep's activities is one of the major functions and similarly one of the major reasons for their under-usage.

**Strategy tools:**

Strategy tools indicate specific procedures, often showing remarkable simplicity combined with high efficiency.

To run a SWOT-analysis with reference to a specific account or DMU will more than pay back.

Experience shows that SWOT-analysis only unleashes its full power, when the four branches carry open questions around Strength, Weaknesses, Opportunities and Threat.

The open questions might vary in case there is no real competitor like it may be the case whit orphan-drugs.

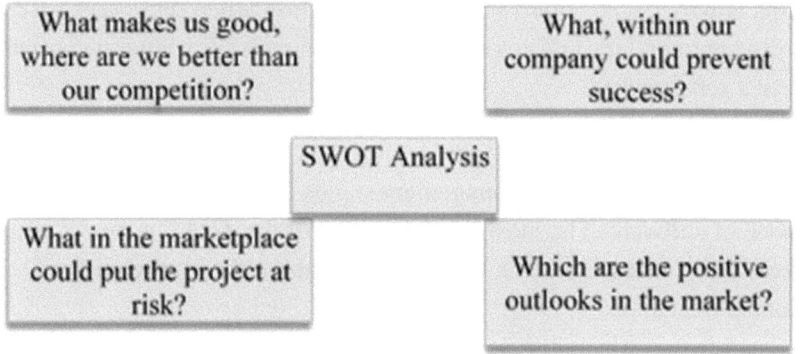

**EXHIBIT 41: SWOT - QUESTIONS**

## SOPs in general

Standard Operating Procedures are omnipresent in pharmaceutical companies. If you look into production or many other areas, you will find SOPs almost everywhere. People working in the respective areas are fully aware of and apply them. Most of these are regularly audited by accounting firms or the FDA. SOPs are taken very seriously. The existence of and the compliance with SOPs in many areas along the value-chain therefore is important for the whole company.

Experience shows that SOPs are often missing in those areas of pharmaceutical companies causing the highest cost and investing the highest budgets: marketing and sales.

## SOP: Lead management

The term "lead" indicates possible and future business. Learning that there may be a qualified lead, must trigger immediate consequences. Otherwise, you may well miss to improve your business as planned. A lead can appear indicating a window of opportunity. It does pay off to create and apply a SOP dealing with "Lead Management." A typical outline of lead management consists of these steps:

- Your KAM runs a range of activities inside the key account.

- Someone in the account or DMU responds, showing interest.

- The KAM collects and captures information about the responding DMU-members and start the following eight step lead-management procedure:

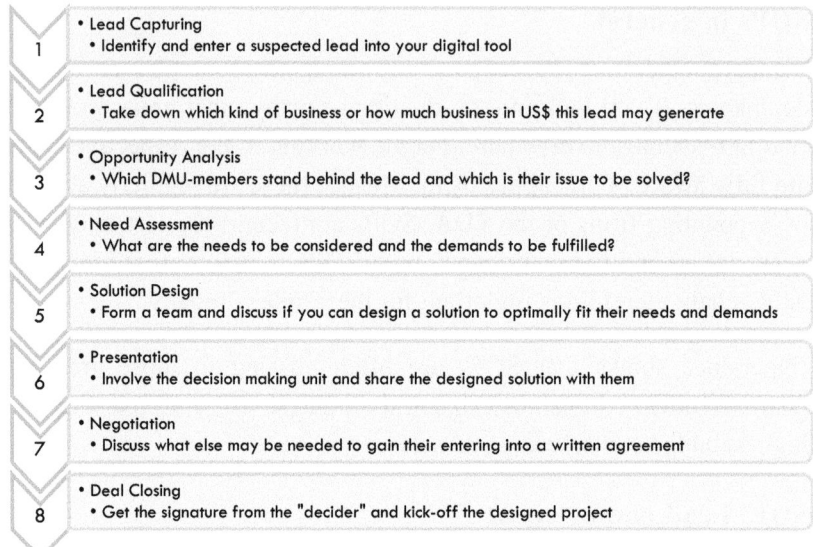

1 • Lead Capturing
  • Identify and enter a suspected lead into your digital tool

2 • Lead Qualification
  • Take down which kind of business or how much business in US$ this lead may generate

3 • Opportunity Analysis
  • Which DMU-members stand behind the lead and which is their issue to be solved?

4 • Need Assessment
  • What are the needs to be considered and the demands to be fulfilled?

5 • Solution Design
  • Form a team and discuss if you can design a solution to optimally fit their needs and demands

6 • Presentation
  • Involve the decision making unit and share the designed solution with them

7 • Negotiation
  • Discuss what else may be needed to gain their entering into a written agreement

8 • Deal Closing
  • Get the signature from the "decider" and kick-off the designed project

**EXHIBIT 42: LEAD MANAGEMENT FLOW OF STEPS**

Following these steps, supported by an accessible, digital tool will allow all concerned to assist and stay informed.

Internal colleagues need to be updated regularly, not only because of budget reasons. They will as well see, which projects can be brought to fruition and which projects fail. Over time your organisation will learn how to contribute and how to add value to such important projects.

Doing something meaningful is one of the major motivational drivers of today's employees. Successfully contributing to Key Account-projects is one of these most rewarding tasks.

## SOP: KAM process

Below graph indicates an overarching flow of steps demonstrating a process to approach Account Management as such.

Behind or underneath every box, there should be a sub-process, reflecting your objectives, your strategy, and your way of doing Key Account Management.

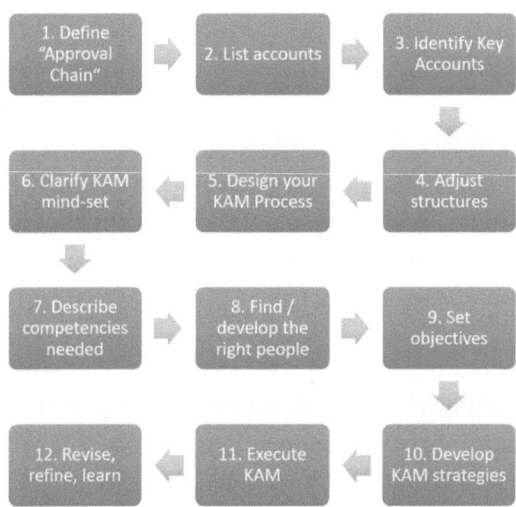

**EXHIBIT 43: THE OVERARCHING KAM-PROCESS**

Drilling every step into more detail will surely pay-off.

# WHERE THE FUTURE LIES

We should not forget the privilege we have, living in the 21$^{st}$ century. At no time in mankind's history human beings have become as old as today and have reached this age in such good health as today. The contribution of the pharmaceutical industry to prolonged and healthier life, and the reduction of infant mortality across the world is undoubtedly remarkable. Pharma positively affects people around the globe. Only few are grateful, and many people, politicians and payers distrust this industry.

## Status quo: it is all about money

Only recently some pharma companies have stepped out of their intended areas of business. Even the Biosimilar business has become a low-price, almost commodity business. Companies are forced to leave their comfort-zones and change. Change is one of the most challenging things to plan.

Companies sometimes have spent years in tracking down a disease and trying to match a possible treatment. At the end, the finishing line already visible, efforts turn out having been in vain.

Stepping out of a market and go for new shores, may have its reason in understanding that the new product will not have a commercial chance in the market. Competitors may already be there, indicating that being just "a me-too" will not pay-off commercially. When clinical differences are little or inexistent, experience in the post-blockbuster era tells, that necessary revenue cannot be achieved. This today even applies to variations of biotechnological drugs.

Yet, there is even another reason of terminating engagements, which constitutes a second issue of pricing. You can see and read about withdrawals from markets when the suggested price is beaten down by payers and assessed to being commercially insufficient. This assessment often connects to pricing issues reaching far beyond a single healthcare system.

In today's globalized world, pricing is something with global effects. In Europe for example, the idea what a healthcare system will pay for a drug, depends on comparisons of prices in other countries. If a drug costs 10 Euro in one country, the neighbor could say, we will only pay 10 Euro minus 20%. The other most common way is price-basketing: the prices of a drug in a defined set of countries is put into a basket, the average calculated and *"The price granted and paid by the tax-funded health system in our country is 50% below the amount of the calculated price-basket."* This means that the (granted) price in one country would harm the pricing in many other countries.

Unprecedented, this price basketing is about to be applied in the US as well.

**Financial toxicity is a threat**

"Financial Toxicity" is a new term. Drugs adding a few weeks to survival from an "otherwise untreatable" condition, costing 10,000 US$ a month are not really the problem. But in many cases and countries patients have to co-pay and in case treated with such a medicine, they will lose all they have. Therapy may be unaffordable.

This situation is leading to a commercial tipping point: the definition of value a medicine might add and the cost of treatment. Financial aspects become toxic. This applies to several treatments of final diseases, but similarly applies to a number of treatments in the area of orphan diseases. Starting at the age of six with a treatment granting a normal life expectancy is fascinating and huge success. The other side of the coin is a one-off treatment costing more than 1 Mio US$ or life-time treatment at more than 100,000 US$ per year. It needs funding, and it does not really make a difference, if an individual pays or a state. The current disconnect between biopharma and payers becomes evident and virulent. The first toxic discussions have already started, when people find that the "cost of goods" are around 100 US$ and the cost of treatment about a thousand times higher.

### Balance sheets show deficits

In financial reports there is a line indicating the "intangible assets". These are defined as non-monetary asset without physical presence. You may take the value of a brand as an intangible asset. You remember the list of the "Top brands of the world" showing skyrocketing values of apple®, Google® etc.

[66]Interestingly enough there is not one pharma company listed in Forbes' list of "The world's most valuable brands". The relation of tangible vs intangible assets has turned upside down in the last

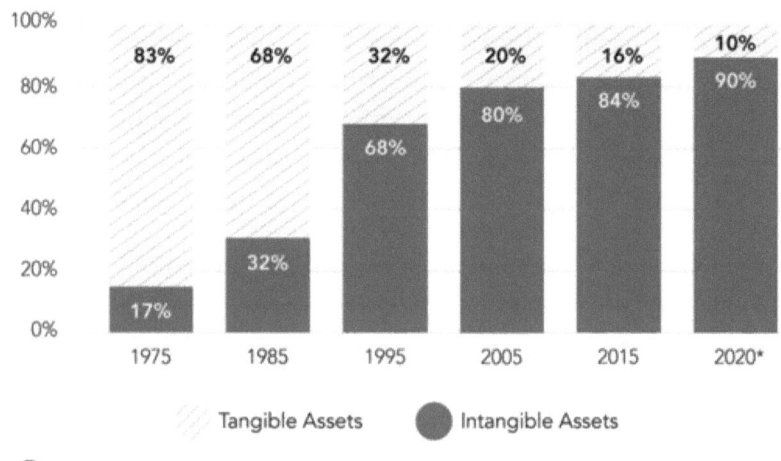

COMPONENTS *of* S&P 500 MARKET VALUE

[66] https://www.oceantomo.com/intangible-asset-market-value-study/

30 years. Today around 90% of the assets are "intangible" in S&P 500 companies. (Source: oceantomo.com)

## A pharma-industry disease

Symptoms are assessed as the basis for a diagnosis. This applies to human ailments and similarly to pharmaceutical companies and their "ailments." A major ailment may be called *greed*. Undoubtedly the Covid-19 pandemic and the great therapeutic achievements brought some points to the positive side on the balance-sheet of this industry. Pharma's profitability ranges in the very top of all industries. Their profit or EBIT-margins are unachievable by most other industries. This is indicative to what may be called *greed*.

Inside many companies and their marketing and sales units, revenue or market share are the predominant parameters. The sales organisation is rewarded by revenue achieved and marketing people fight for omni-channel efficiency. It all appears to be about money in most cases. These questions may be asked to the board and the stock-exchange.

- Did the powerful PR-machine around annual press conferences ever communicate the *number of patients* successfully treated with a drug?

- Did you ever hear in an annual press conference the "burden of disease" reduced by a company's drugs?

- Did you ever read about the improvement of "quality of life" only close or even next to the financial statements?

- Where is the value delivered by pharma and who delivers?

- As long as this industry is seen as a money printing machine, this industry will fail to deliver anything even close to "patient-centricity".

The visible symptom of "commercial greed" you can see on the desk of almost each medical representative: the sales target set and to be achieved, is indicated and marked in commercial figures.

They have to achieve a specific revenue for a named product. They are still called sales-people, fully ignoring the fact that they do not sell, since a doctor does not buy. Their task still is called "selling" and they are not even expected to "serve" doctors or patients.

## Sell or Serve

A pharma industry "selling" their products to prescribers or hospitals creates questions. The key ones are those around delivering value. Pharma assumedly is the last industry, sending myriads of "salespeople" to make unsolicited and unannounced calls to doctors, pharmacists, hospitals, and other healthcare providers. Often, they are trained to simply hammer a promotional message and at the end request the doctor to prescribe their product. The pandemic interfered heavily, but the search goes for alternative channels, not for structural change.

Doctors by profession are philanthropists and usually educated well enough to endure sales calls and suffer in silence. One consequence is that after the mental doors have closed already, the physical doors of doctors over time are closing too.

The problem lies in the resilience of pharma's omnipresent commercial mentality, old fashioned concepts, and the evident inability to change, so far. The fact that pharma is highly regulated and incestuous when it comes to their employees, only adds to the tragedy. Pharma still is in selling drugs. Intangible assets beyond patents? Negative.

The vast majority of drugs today is generic, and many countries already have started to request or only allow INN-prescriptions. Who believes that there is an informational need from a physician around a molecule which is around 10 or 15 years, will have to admit that "drug-information" definitely or hardly is a relevant topic. If information about half-life and evasion time etc. is not really an option, what could then be the option for pharma? In any case, it was and will never be "selling" drugs and be very clear that "customer" definitely is a commercially wrong and professionally inappropriate term for a physician. Prescribing physicians are not pharma's customers.

## HIDDEN TREASURES IN PHARMA

A pharmaceutical company is a complex organism, carrying a semantic legacy as a burden: the terms *department* and *division* still exist. Both terms, *department* and *division* have their origin in early industrialisation. Both terms indicate the opposite of collaboration.

Introducing the term "Business Unit" points into the direction of working together, a "conditio, sine qua non" for success in today's world.

If a company wants to strive for patient orientation, cross-departmental collaboration is a "must". Departments like medical, research and development, those who run clinical trials, galenics, production, distribution, and logistics need to contribute. Their individual expertise will add a lot of value in support of the work of Key Account Managers.

### Medical and treatment expertise

There is no other place where all this comprehensive knowledge and expertise about a specific disease lies, as in a pharmaceutical company. Pitifully all this treasure is hidden in medical and research departments, archives, literature databases and inside the reports of clinical trials.

Not only are there bright brains available, but vast knowledge about the disease, problems patients have, solutions to enhance therapy adherence and many other aspects of disease and their treatment.

## Problem solving instead of pill-pushing

No one has better insight into clinics and doctor's offices than pharmaceutical reps who intimately know many surgeries. They could, and many do, know about the time constraints of a doctor and they could assist to improve this problem, since they know the differences between many doctors. Reps will know how to attract patients to an office and they could have ideas how to keep them related and referred to this doctor's office.

We all are in the middle of the digital revolution and many HCPs do or cannot take the time which is needed to save them time. Why could reps not be trained to assist? Of course, we must not forget the patients. They suffer and some companies keep telling the world, they stand in the middle. Reality often tells a different story.

Imagine there are 10 companies offering the same Telmisartan or Meloxicam. This is normal. Which generic would be used more often: the one from a company "selling drugs to doctors" or the competitor who offers a complex approach ensuring better patient outcome by improving drug adherence?

The second provider would be most welcome and of course deliver better value to every single doctor, the payer, patients, the patient's relatives and next of kin and anyone else affected and concerned.

*The commercial success will follow the value delivered. It never is the other way round!*

Many of these medical representatives could add insight and value to Key Account Management. They only need to be involved and engaged in designing solutions, reaching far "beyond the pill." Once Key Account Management is internally perceived as a cross-functional approach, serving patients, their healthcare providers, and many others involved in improving patient's health and well-being.

Key Account Management will pave the way to novel concepts and foster the readiness of pharma to actively engage in the delivery of care.

Once conceptually agreed, KAM will add real value to the marketplace and deliver massive benefits by improving patient outcome.

As an intended side-effect, KAM will allow this great industry to improve their reputation and still be commercially successful.

**Delivering value is where the future lies.**

# EPILOGUE

*Indeed, 'beyond the pill' is rapidly becoming an established norm; it is what pharma can do to encourage people to take up the challenges of self-care and become active participants in their health and well-being.* (Jane Ayton & Jane Barrett, 2014)

The future will show less and less space for an industry "simply" providing interchangeable commodities at the best price.

The need to improve healthcare outcome and raise healthcare efficiency in developed or mature markets is high and rising.

The unmet medical need today is a scarce source granting a future for many pharmaceutical companies.

The need to make healthcare achievable for the poor, stands for cost-containment and promotes mass production of cheap generics.

Providing access to medical care and treatment options for people living in remote rural areas is a must, to stop urbanization, making sure that agricultural production will continue feeding the people.

Raising political barriers for pharmaceutical companies, whose central interest is making money, evidently will continue.

On the other hand, the pharmaceutical industry bears and stores enormous knowledge about their respective disease areas. Pitifully, the traditional business-model prevents pharma from making this huge treasure available.

A comprehensive offering to solve or improve any of those needs and demands will assumedly be most rewarding. The first examples are visible.

Creating something "beyond the pill" is not really easy to achieve. It needs a lot of courage, shareholder's support, and creativity.

New competitors are emerging in form of information technology. Mobile Health, telehealth, mini- and nanochips, therapeutic apps, and many other applications are available already. They all are competing for patients.

Change is everywhere. Darwin's sentence about the survival of the fittest must be replaced by "the survival of those, most adaptive to change."

**The introduction of KAM, in pursuit of building and sustaining a robust and lasting relationship to improve delivery of healthcare, is one way to provide appreciated value to all involved.**

Professionally designed and executed Key Account Management will prevent the pharmaceutical industry from being degraded playing the role as a simple and replaceable supplier of commodities.

*April 2021*

# LIST OF REFERENCES

Andris A. Zoltners, P. S. (2014, 10 19). *HBR blogs*. Retrieved from Harvard Business Review: http://blogs.hbr.org/2014/09/sales-data-only-matters-if-it-helps-you-take-action/?utm_source=feedburner&utm_medium=feed&utm_campaign=Feed%3A+harvardbusiness+%28HBR.org%29

Barclay, R. (2014, January 23). *Healthline*. Retrieved from Sugar levels in tears: http://www.healthline.com/health-news/diabetes-google-develops-glucose-monitoring-contact-lens-012314

Björn Ivens, Catherine Pardo;. (2014). *The Role of Key Account Management in Marketing and Sales Intelligence*. www.ifm.unisg.ch/weiterbildung: Springer für Professionals | Marketing.

BMJ 2014;348:g3169 . (2014, 08 01). *http://www.bmj.com/content/348/bmj.g3169*. Retrieved from www.BMJ.com.

Capgemini Consulting. (2012). *Estimated Annual Pharmaceutical Revenue Loss due to Medication Non-Adherence*.

Cegedim. (2010). *The Cegedim Market Access Industry Report*. Boulogne - Billancourt, F: Cegedim.

Coleman, J. S. (1966). Medical Innovation. A diffusion study.

Coleman, J. S., Katz, E., & Menzel, H. (1966). Medical Innovation. A diffusion study. p. 179 ff.

Cooper, K. (2014, 06 22). *http://blogs.rollcall.com/moneyline/drug-companies-give-million-dollar-boost-to-lobbying/?dcz=* .

Dan Pink. (2014, June 6). *ted.com*. Retrieved from http://www.ted.com/talks/dan_pink_on_motivation/transcript

David Laws, @eyeforpharma. (2014, June 13). *Industry Healthcheck 2014*. Retrieved from EyeForPharma: http://www.eyeforpharma.com/download/content-healthcheck.php

EMA. (2014, 10 8). *Eruopean Medicines Agency*. Retrieved from Abut Us:
http://www.ema.europa.eu/ema/index.jsp?curl=pages/about_us/general/gen
eral_content_000235.jsp&mid=

Ernest&Young. (2014). *EY | Progressions Global Pharmaceutical Report*.
www.ey.com/progressions2014: Ernest & Young.

Etymonline. (2014, 11 3). *Etymonline*. Retrieved from www.Etymonline.com:
http://www.etymonline.com/index.php?allowed_in_frame=0&search=mind
set&searchmode=none

Fiercepharma. (2010, 1 25). *Pharma plowed millions into Q4 lobbying*. Retrieved
from Fiercepharma: www.fiercepharma.com/...y/pharma-plowed-millions-
q4-lobbying/2010-01-25?utm_medium=nl&utm_source=internal

Forissier, T., & Katrina Firlik, M. (2014, June 26). Retrieved from
www.capgemini.com: http://www.capgemini.com/resource-file-
access/resource/pdf/Estimated_Annual_Pharmaceutical_Revenue_Loss_Du
e_to_Medication_Non-Adherence.pdf

IMS-Institute. (2012). *The benefits of responsible use of medicines - Setting policies
for better and cost-effective healthcare.*

Jane Ayton & Jane Barrett. (2014). *Power to the people.*
http://www.pmlive.com/pharma_news/power_to_the_people_an_era_of_se
lf-care_612747: PMLive.

Kotler, P. (2008). *Marketing Management.*

Kotter, J. P. (2002). *The heart of change.* http://www.kotterinternational.com/the-8-
step-process-for-leading-change/.

Kotter, J. P. (2003). Leading Change - Why transformation efforts fail. *Harvard
Business Review.*

Kotter, John P. (2014, 12 10). *The 8-Step Process for Leading Change.* Retrieved
from KotterInternational: http://www.kotterinternational.com/the-8-step-
process-for-leading-change/

Mauborgne, R., & Kim, C. (2009). How Strategy Shapes Structure. *Harvard
Business Review.*

Meek, T. (2014, January 30). *PMLIve.* Retrieved from www.PMLive.com: http://www.pmlive.com/pharma_news/novo_partners_with_nhs_on_diabet es_care_538752

Paul Simms, C. e. (2014). *Industry Healthcheck 2014.*

PMLive.com; Kirstie Pickering. (2014, October 7). *PMLive.com.* Retrieved from http://www.pmlive.com/pharma_news/uk_biotech_leaders_partner_on_scie nce_lobbying_604691

Porter, M. E., & Lee, T. H. (2013, September 18). The strategy that will fix healthcare. Harvard Business Review blog.

Profeta, S. (2014, 07 10). *Virtual Sanity.* Retrieved from http://profeta.dk/blog/2012/05/09/b2b-customer-centricity/

Quintiles, Value is the target. (2014, February 7). *Value is the target.* Retrieved from http://www.quintiles.com/library/white-papers/value-is-the-target

Rubicon. (2014, July 20). *Rubicon.* Retrieved from www.rubiconv2r.com: http://www.rubiconv2r.com/news/new-infographic-illustrates-the-rubicon-white-paper-on-becoming-a-kam-organisation

Stacy, M. (2014, June 23). For Breakthrough Innovation, Focus on Possibility, Not Profitability. Harvard Business Review Blog. Retrieved from http://blogs.hbr.org/2014/06/for-breakthrough-innovation-focus-on-possibility-not-profitability/?utm_source=feedburner&utm_medium=feed&utm_campaign =Feed%3A+harvardbusiness+%28HBR.org%29

Steve Kerr, HBR. (2014, August 27). *Harvard Business Review.* Retrieved from blogs.hbr.org: http://blogs.hbr.org/2014/08/do-your-companys-incentives-reward-bad-behavior/?utm_source=feedburner&utm_medium=feed&utm_campaign=F eed%3A+harvardbusiness+%28HBR.org%29

Thomas Forissier, K. F. (2012). *Estimated Annual Pharmaceutical Revenue Loss.* Cap Gemini Consulting.

Tom Peters. (1979). *Beyond the matrix.* McKinsey.

Tyer, D., & Pickering, K. (2014). *Sales reps struggle to access doctors.*
http://www.pmlive.com
/pharma_intelligence/sales_reps_struggle_to_access_doctors_601905:
PMLive.

W. Scott Evangelista, Deloitte. (2009). *Fiercepharma.* Retrieved from
http://fiercepharma.com

Wells, B. (2014, August 14). NHS in Scotland deploys mobile healthcare.
http://www.pharmafile.com/print/192372.

*Wikipedia.* (2014, 10 20). Retrieved from http://en.wikipedia.org/:
http://en.wikipedia.org/wiki/Business_process

Wikipedia. (2014, 10 21). Retrieved from
http://en.wikipedia.org/wiki/Management_by_objectives

*Wikipedia.* (2014, 10 22). Retrieved from http://en.wikipedia.org/wiki/Management

Wikipedia. (2014, July 11). *http://www.en.wikipedia.org.* Retrieved from
http://en.wikipedia.org/wiki/Customer

Wikipedia. (2020, March 2). Retrieved from www.en.Wikipedia.org:
http://en.wikipedia.org/wiki/Health_maintenance_organization

Wolfram, Hanno. (2014, October 4). *MedicinMan India.* Retrieved from
http://medicinman.net/2014/10/october-2014-issue/

worldwide, National Analysts, booz&co . (2012). *Pharmaceutical Sales and
Marketing Trends 2011.* Website: Booz & Company -.

# LIST OF EXHIBITS

## Acknowledgements

This book is the summarized knowledge and experience from many consulting, change projects and workshops in more than 25 countries with pharmaceutical companies.

"The more you teach, the more you learn." is what I found enormously enriching. Thanks to all those who contributed to discussions, shared their experience and their individual wealth of wisdom.

Thanks to my wife Ulrike for the patience, she had.

Thanks to my friend Winfried Heyland, who helped a lot making the graphs looking sufficiently professional